Email Users Handbook

Email Users Handbook

A Beginner's Guide

by GRANT BURNS

McFarland & Company, Inc., Publishers
Jefferson, North Carolina, and London

Library of Congress Cataloguing-in-Publication Data

Burns, Grant, 1947–
    Email users handbook : a beginner's guide / by Grant Burns.
        p.   cm.
    Includes index.

    ISBN 0-7864-1421-9 (softcover : 50# alkaline paper)

    1. Electronic mail messages—Handbooks, manuals, etc.   2. Electronic
mail systems—Handbooks, manuals, etc.   I. Title.
HE7551.B87   2002
004.692—dc21   2002007624

British Library cataloguing data are available

Cover image ©2002 PhotoSpin

Manufactured in the United States of America

McFarland & Company, Inc., Publishers
  Box 611, Jefferson, North Carolina 28640
   www.mcfarlandpub.com

Table of Contents

Introduction

Email (short for "electronic mail") is a wonderful invention. It allows you to send messages via the Internet across town, across the country, and around the world, easily, efficiently, and inexpensively. Email is extremely versatile. You can use it for serious business correspondence, for personal notes, for continuing exchanges with friends, relatives, or complete strangers on topics that concern and interest you. You can use email to contact government officials, including, as a rule, your congressional representatives, United States senators, and state office holders. If you're a student, you can contact your teachers or professors.

With email, you can send messages of praise, complaint, or inquiry to corporate customer service representatives. You can send letters to the editors of newspapers and magazines. You can save on your telephone bill by keeping in email contact with your college student children, your parents, grandparents, or distant friends. With email, depending on the circumstances of the message, you may be as concise as a telegram, or as discursive as a long, chatty letter. Email, by far the most popular activity on the Internet, is a terrific tool, and almost anyone can use it.

How Long Has Email Been Around?

According to Steven Anzovin's and Janet Podell's revision of Joseph Nathan Kane's standard reference work *Famous First Facts* (H.W. Wilson, 2000), the first electronic mail message occurred in 1972 when computer engineer Ray Tomlinson sent an email—to himself. Tomlinson, who worked with BBN Technologies (now part of GTE), was testing the ARPANET's messaging capabilities. ARPANET was the American military forerunner of the Internet. We don't know quite what Tomlinson wrote; presumably not "Mr. Tomlinson, come here, I want you." Alexander Graham Bell's descendants probably still have a patent on that one. Traffic has picked up considerably since Tomlinson was talking to himself back in '72: The Internet market research firm eMarketer reported in 2000 that people send over 1.6 billion noncommercial email messages each day in the United States alone. That is almost three times the number of first-class conventional mailings.

Are You Really Inexperienced?

Then this book is for you. If you picked it up hoping that it would help you take advantage of the wonderful invention of email, I hope you find it just what you need to get you started in this enjoyable, efficient, and largely free form of communication.

I do not intend this guide for experienced Internet users. I don't mean it for people who download a dozen shareware files before breakfast, talk in initialisms (IMHO, ROTFL and other insider gibberish), and taught themselves programming on a Timex Sinclair with a membrane keyboard. (I have one of those in the original box in a closet somewhere; that 2K memory was quite the pip!)

This book really is for beginners, for those folks who want to be part of the email scene, but who are not sure how to get started—and might be afraid to ask. It's for people who would like to send emails to their distant family members or friends, but have never gotten around to browsing the how-to books in the computer literature section of the nearest bookstore or library.

There are tons (probably literally) of books on computer how-to. These books often intimidate the newcomer, with hundreds of pages, indexes crammed with teeny-tiny type, and far more details than anyone needs to know to establish an email account, send and receive messages, and keep reasonable track of them. Most of these books serve good purposes, but too often they drive the raw recruit back to the fiction or gardening sections.

Some books that might help can put potential readers off because of their titles. If you're feeling a little anxious about your lack of computer skills, but have some basic self-respect, you might not be inclined to walk up to the bookstore cashier or the library loan desk with a book whose cover is emblazoned with a title like *Computers for Morons*. Yet there are many such books, with many such titles. The books are sometimes very good, once you get past the covers, but the tongue-in-cheek titles can wound those already sensitive about their unsophisticated computer abilities.

Let's clear up one fallacy right off the bat: No one needs more than a smidgen of "computer literacy" to use email. This is not rocket science. No, I'll take that back. It might be something like rocket science on the end where computer geniuses figure out how to make these systems work. Nevertheless, as a grandmother in Grand Forks who wants to be able to correspond by email with her college-student granddaughter, you no more need to know how email systems work behind the scenes than you need to know how the automatic transmission in your car has enough sense to shift from second to third gear when you get up to the proper speed. As long as it shifts when it should, what does it matter why and how? If it doesn't, that's a problem for the folks at your favorite garage.

Getting on the Mail Wagon

A survey from the UCLA Center for Communication Policy indicated not long ago that over half the citizens of the United States use email. Of the four in 10 or so who do not, many have not enjoyed much in the way of opportunities to learn how to use computers even for the easiest and most enjoyable purpose. That purpose, in my opinion, is keeping in touch with the people you care about, and who share your interests in the things of the world.

Email is easy. Anyone who can read and type (two-finger hunting & pecking will do) can learn the basics in a short time. I know, though, that many people seize up when they come within arm's length of a computer keyboard and monitor. I spend a fair chunk of my time working at a university library reference desk. Even there, in an environment that places a huge emphasis on work with computers, I meet many people who approach the hardware with trepidation.

"I'm not very computer literate" is a statement that I hear every week, usually several times a week, from people who are afraid to throw themselves into the library computers for fear something will grab them and not let them back out. Or that they might "break" something. Sometimes I hear this line from younger library users, but more often from students returning to college after many years away. These folks, in their thirties, forties, and older (sometimes much older), did not grow up with a computer in the house, as so many of their younger classmates did. They never saw a computer in their elementary or high schools, they do not work with them, and, if they were to speak frankly, they would say that what the things do seems like incomprehensible magic. Let me confess: Sometimes its seems that way to me, too.

Another group, which sometimes intersects with the one I just described, has never enjoyed the financial means to have a computer in the home. If we judged by television and the movies, we would think that absolutely everyone has a state-of-the-art computer somewhere around the house—maybe in the study down the hall from the home theater, which, of course, we all also have.

It isn't true. A new computer and its "peripherals" (equipment like a printer and a monitor) cost anywhere from around $700 to much, much more than that. For a single mother paying her own college tuition and working as a clerk in a discount department store, that 700 bucks has a lot of work to do more important than plunking a new Dell with the latest Pentium chip down on the desk in the corner of the living room. For a couple with three young children, an '87 Buick Century as their "reliable" vehicle (that's what I drive every day), and two minimum wage jobs, the only apple under the Christmas tree will probably be the kind that grew on a tree itself. For a retiree living on a fixed income, with monthly prescription bills that are anything but fixed, a home computer might well be out of the question.

If you saw yourself anywhere in the above paragraphs, take heart. Whatever your personal situation, it's probably going to be easier for you to join the computer world than you think. Much easier. It will be a lot of fun. And the really good part is that you don't have to own a computer to do it.

Check It Out at the Library

I have focused for the most part in this book on email systems that almost anyone can use free of charge. The only requirement is that you be able to use a computer with access to the Internet, including the Web. If you do not have a computer in the home, your best bet is your public library. More and more libraries are finding that it makes good sense, from several points of view, to encourage their users to take full advantage of the Web, including use of email, from library computer workstations.

There are exceptions, of course. Some librarians have not yet loosened up sufficiently that seeing patrons doing email doesn't disturb their sense of scholarly propriety. They think that such business isn't "serious," or it has nothing to do with "research," and that it gets in the way of the truly studious types who would be soaking up online encyclopedia articles on 19th century women poets with three names (or four, maybe) if only those emailers wouldn't hog the workstations.

Well, pshaw. I would encourage some of my professional colleagues to expand their field of view a little, and let the people have their way. I agree: no computer games on the reference room terminals. That is taking liberties a bit far. But email? Why not? As Karen G. Schneider said in her article "Internet Librarian: You've Got Mail" (*American Libraries*, June/July 1999), "In the name of good customer service, public relations, and service to the underserved, don't just open the door to email—welcome your patrons, ungrudgingly." Schneider advocates point-of-use instruction in email in the library, and points out that "Free email at the local library is an obvious boon to people who do not own computers or have personal Internet accounts."

Misgivings will not disappear because of a couple of quotes from an enthusiastic people's librarian, but Schneider is not alone in her advocacy. In her article "E-Mail for Everyone: Free from Your Friendly Librarian" (*Searcher*, Jan. 2001), Irene E. McDermott echoes Schneider. She does note evolving objections to permitting public emailing on library machines, including problems with resident programs on computers (imagine patron downloads to the library hard drives—eeyew!).

Web email comes close to solving the problem. McDermott acknowledges that a patron could inadvertently download a virus through Web mail and free it to run wild in a hard drive, but that can happen through other Web procedures, not just email. If library patrons have open access to the Web—and why wouldn't they?—there's a world of trouble out there just itching to take a seat in library computers.

McDermott counsels calm. Calm, and "strong, regularly updated antivirus software." If your library's computers lack protection from such programs as Norton AntiVirus or McAfee VirusScan, it is time to get them squared away.

With my neophyte audience in mind, I have tried to keep things as simple and straightforward as possible here. The book marches through a number of the best-known Web-based email systems, as well as four prominent standalone systems that can be downloaded at no charge on one's home computer. For each system I have covered the basics: sending messages, retrieving messages, filing messages in folders, working with attachments and address books, and so on. This is meat & potatoes computing: simple fare, but I hope, nourishing and easily digested. Anyone who reads the book from front to back will see some repetition in the kinds of advice it offers; that follows from my decision to set it up so that a given reader could read only Part One and one other section (on Hotmail, say), not bother with the rest, and yet not miss out on anything of major importance. The book's objective is to get new users into email, quickly and easily, with a little background orientation.

At some point, every computer user is brand-new to the game. There is nothing wrong with that. There is nothing to be ashamed of in not knowing how to do email, or any other computer application. Again, it does not take marvelous technological skills to use email. Anyone can learn. Even you, no matter how flummoxed you may feel when you get close to one of those infernal machines.

Come on. Let me show you.

PART ONE

Getting to Know Email

1. *What You Need to Get Started*

If you're going to do email from home, you'll need:

A computer, a monitor, and a keyboard
A phone line
A modem. (Ask for a "56K"; that's as fast as you'll get on the modem front, and it won't cost you much more than a slower modem). A modem enables your computer to use your telephone line to send and receive data, rather than voice.

An Internet Service Provider (ISP). Check your local yellow pages under "Internet On-Line Service Providers." Unless you're living in a rural area or small town, there should be several listed. Talk with at least a couple of them to see what kinds of plans they have. Ask friends and acquaintances for recommendations. People who have had good, or bad, experiences with their ISPs will be delighted to give you the details. Today, a typical ISP will charge you $20–$30 a month for unlimited access to the Internet and the World Wide Web. (The Web is part of the Internet, not the other way around.) You'll want to be sure that you're dialing into a local number supplied by your ISP, not into a long-distance number.

If you live out in the boondocks, with no local Internet number, you might inquire about MCI WorldCom's MCI Mail. The company offers toll-free access to its electronic mail service. You can reach MCI Mail at 800-444-6245. Access, as noted, is free; the service is not a freebie. According to the currently-posted MCI Mail price structure, there's a minimum monthly charge of $10, an annual fee of $35, and—here's where verbose types could run up a bill—a fee for every message sent, based on the number of characters in the message (the first 500 characters cost 50 cents).

There are other forms of connection to the Internet, including WebTV, cable, and digital subscription lines (DSL). Dwelling on these is beyond the scope of this guide. Visit your library's or your local good bookstore's popular computing section, and you will probably find many books that will tell you how these systems work. (Try not to let titles that include words like "Dummies" and "Idiots" put you off.)

Oh, and you also need an email program. Your ISP will most likely offer you one, and an email address. Additionally, you can sign up at no charge with one of the systems covered in this guide. There are many other free email programs; if you would like to investigate other possible programs, there are a number of Web sites that will help you choose. Two good possibilities suggested by Irene McDermott (and functional as of December, 2001):

The Free Email Providers Guide, *http://www.fepg.net*, offers leads to more than 1,300 free email providers. More than a mere list, this guide contains much useful information, and helps prospective provider users compare features through an easy-to-read table format. The Free Email Address Directory, at *http://www.emailaddresses.com*, also lists well over 1,000 free email services. It provides links to helpful articles about free email, as well as lots of other agreeable online aids.

Basic Email Systems

The common types of email delivery are standalone, or client-based, systems like Eudora and Outlook Express, and Web-based systems, like Hotmail and Yahoo! Client-based systems employ a POP3 (Post Office Protocol Version3) or an IMAP (Internet Message Access Protocol) server. A POP3 server is a potent computer that receives and sorts email, and gives it to a client computer (the one in your basement, perhaps) on demand. The IMAP server enables more flexible interaction with its client computers. The client computer uses the SMTP (Simple Mail Transfer Protocol) to send mail.

Standalone systems have more features than Web-based mail systems, and can store vast amounts of email, far more than Web systems. They are the best systems for those who anticipate doing a very large quantity of email transactions, such as those resulting from a business. Web-based systems, on the other hand, are great for frequent travelers, because they allow full access from any computer where one can reach the Internet—from one's basement office computer in Cleveland to a public library Web workstation in Omaha, to a cyber café computer in Seattle. With a Web-based system, there is nothing to buy; most of these systems are easy to learn; and their features will satisfy the great majority of personal email users. The drawback, of course, is that one must go to a place that offers public Web access if one does not own a computer and have an Internet account.

No Computer? Go Web.

Web-based systems are the obvious choice for those who do not have home computers. They can also be a plus for those working in institutional computing environments. Workplace email systems, and the messages on them, are the property of the employer, who can read those messages if so inclined. A corporate worker with Web access can gain privacy through using one of the Web email systems. There is, however, no such thing as complete email security in any environment, regardless of what system one uses. Computer monitoring techniques available to system managers are well advanced, and the level of surveillance of employee computing activities in the workplace is not always clearly communicated to those being monitored. If you send personal emails in your workplace, try to do so with an awareness of the house rules, and exercise discretion. "Flaming" your CEO's intelligence or ancestry through email on company time, whether through the company system or via an independent Web email system, is not in tune with your enlightened self-interest.

To use any of the email programs described in this guide, you must have a Web browser installed on your machine. The most popular browsers are Netscape and Microsoft's Internet Explorer. Both these browsers may be obtained free by downloading from the Web. For a modest charge ($10 for Internet Explorer, less than that for Netscape), you may also order them on CD-ROM from their producers. To obtain Netscape, go to *http://netscape.com/* and click the little New Download button near the page's upper-right corner. That will take you to a page from which you can order or download the latest version of Netscape, or other Netscape browsers. To order or download Internet Explorer, go to: *http://www.microsoft.com/windows/ie/ downloads/default.asp.*

If you bought a new computer any time in the last several years, it almost surely came with a browser already installed on it. If you do not have a computer (or at the least, WebTV) at home, your best bet for Web access is your public library.

With your computer and modem properly set up, and your account established with your ISP, you dial into the ISP through your modem. The ISP then turns you loose on the Internet to do what you will. Alternatively, you can sign up with an online service rather than with an ISP. America Online is the best known in this area. Such online services can be handy for beginning Internet users, but they have limitations that you may eventually want to escape by going with an ISP.

2. *Booking the Web at the Library*

Some libraries require that you reserve time on their Web-access computers. The Web is incredibly popular, and many public libraries find themselves swamped with computer users, a large number of whom go nowhere near the book collections. Librarians often find it necessary to establish some ground rules on computer use. Your local public library might not require reservations, but if you call before visiting, you can find out; you can also ask when traffic will be lightest, thus enhancing your chances of securing a spot at a machine if reservations are not the local rule.

I have lightly chided librarians for sometimes having what I think is an unreasonable aversion to patron use of library computers for email. Speaking as a librarian, let me suggest that you, the emailer, observe the regulations your library has set up for computer use. If the signs say, for example, "Please limit your computer use to 30 minutes at a time," do not sit there at the keyboard for two hours. ("Tempus fugit," as my old high school Latin teacher used to say on a daily basis. "Time flies," and it flies with amazing rapidity when you're online. Keep an eye on the clock!) Patrons who routinely and egregiously ignore posted rules and verbal requests do not endear themselves to library staff, who have other patrons to serve with needs that are probably as urgent as those of the folks who seem to be cemented to their chairs at the Web workstations.

If you have special circumstances that do not fit well into your library's rules, talk to the reference librarian on duty and explain your situation. Ask if there is another arrangement you could work out with the library. If your needs are evident and reasonable, the library might make an exception to one rule or another to help you accomplish your objectives. But get this business squared away before the fact, rather than trying to do so after you have tied up a machine for half the morning and were finally asked to yield to someone else. Librarians are, by and large, a fairly accommodating bunch, but they appreciate an opportunity to solve special patron problems and needs at the front end, rather than trying to clean up a mess after the fact.

What About College Libraries?

Public libraries have been the emphasis above. The degree of welcome you experience in your efforts to use computers in a college or university library, as someone not affiliated with the institution, will vary considerably. Many academic libraries allow only very limited use of their computers to those who are not current students, faculty, or staff of their host institutions. You might find that your nearby college library computers are set up so that, to reach anything but the library's catalog, you must log in with a user name and a password on the campus system. As someone not affiliated with the school, you will not be able to do so—even as an alumnus.

That sort of restriction is not as unfriendly and unreasonable as it may seem at first glance. Sure, you're a taxpayer. If your local college is publicly supported, part of the support comes from you. Even so, your support as a taxpayer is miniscule compared to the tuition and fees that the school's students pay every semester. Those students really do deserve primary consideration regarding campus computing services, including the library's. It simply does not do to make a student who pays thousands of dollars in tuition, and who needs to do online research for a term paper, twiddle her thumbs while someone from the public at large reads the newspaper sports section or sends gossipy emails at the library Web station she would like to use.

The missions of academic and public libraries are very different, and account for great variations in the kinds of privileges members of the general public enjoy in them. If your local college library does feel able to offer Web access to those not affiliated with the school, be scrupulous about observing any posted rules or verbal requests from the staff. That will go far to improve the chances of the privilege continuing. If the library changes its policy, however, and you find that you can no longer gain Web access there, do not be shocked. Academic libraries are under intense pressure from numerous quarters—not the least of which are campus information technology authorities concerned about security—to make sure that students, faculty, and academic staff do not have to compete with the general public for computing opportunities.

3. Notes for Handicapped Emailers (and the librarians who help them)

Many people who would like to send and receive email face some obstacles other than lack of a computer, or of a nearby library that encourages its patrons to use email on its workstations. Arthritis or neurological problems can make typing slow, and can render using a conventional mouse all but impossible. Poor vision can make reading the information on a computer monitor a major challenge. Fortunately, some recourse does exist to make the emailing experience easier for these folks.

One of the least expensive solutions, for people who have trouble manipulating a mouse, is the trackball. A trackball takes the place of a mouse, and, in fact, looks rather like one—but with a ball in it that the user rolls around to position the cursor on the screen. Another alternative to the mouse is the touch pad (like the Easy Cat touch pad available from Options by Infogrip, Inc.), which allows cursor control with only a slight finger movement; the user can simply drag his or her finger across the pad. The Deskstick (also from Options by Infogrip) is a mouse emulator that relies on finger pressure. It frees the user from having to make repetitive, stressful hand motions. You'll find Infogrip on the Web at *http://www.infogrip.com* (800-397-0921).

Keyboard technology has also made strides toward meeting the needs of computer users who find standard set-ups awkward or unusable. The Tash WinMini keyboard is a small, pressure-sensitive keyboard with membrane keys; it is available with a standard key layout, or with the most frequently-used letters in the keyboard's center; this layout helps cut down on fatigue. The keyboard allows the user to control both keyboard and mouse functions. Tash, Inc. is at *http://www.tashinc.com*. The keyboard is not inexpensive, however, with a current list price of $750.

A recent entry in the keyboard line comes from a new company, Finger-Works (*http://www.fingerworks.com*). The Finger-Works keyboard, dubbed the TouchStream, employs sensors that respond to very light touch. Finger-Works also provides a substitute for the functions of an ordinary mouse by enabling finger gestures anywhere on the iGesture Pad to give mouse commands to the computer. The Finger-Works product line stemmed from founder Dr. Wayne Westerman's frustration at being unable to use a standard keyboard and mouse because of repetitive stress difficulties with his hands. Prices are not outrageous: The basic TouchStream keyboard costs about $200; the iGesture Pad goes for about $190.

People who use wheelchairs generally have their homes set up to meet their unique needs, but, in spite of the Americans with Disabilities Act, they continue to contend with public facilities that simply do not measure up to their requirements—sometimes in spite of good-faith efforts to anticipate these requirements. In the recently built library where I work, architects and designers tried to foresee handicapped users' needs. The building has, for example, an adequate number of carrels intended for handicapped students and other handicapped library users.

Unfortunately, none of these carrels has a work surface high enough to allow a student with his motorized wheelchair and its vertical control arm to slide his legs under comfortably: All the work surfaces are about an inch too low. Working with one of our campus student services people, we're bringing in a specially built table to accommodate this student.

If you are a librarian, you'll need to be alert to possible solutions for a wide range of handicapped access problems. As Bonnie Vaccarella observes in "Finding Our Way through the Maze of Adaptive Technology" (*Computers in Libraries*, Oct. 2001), it is important to consult handicapped users themselves about their needs. No matter how sincerely one tries to walk in the shoes, or roll in the wheelchairs, of handicapped patrons, it is often impossible to grasp the subtle details of what works and what does not work for them, unless you hear it from the handicapped themselves.

If you are a handicapped library user, do not hesitate to make your needs known to library staff. Do not assume that a situation that doesn't work for you is bound to stay that way because no one cares. Chances are good that, rather than not caring, no one has thought about the problem because it has not been brought to attention by anyone who directly experiences it. Librarians are usually ready to do their best to help, but sometimes they have to be told just what sort of help their patrons need.

Returning to specific handicaps, visual problems are probably the greatest single impediment to effective computer use. These, too, can often be addressed. Sometimes the cure is simple, easy, and cost-free, such as adjusting the font size in monitor displays. I have seen library computer monitors whose standard print display is ridiculously tiny. Increasing the font size can mean the difference between some users having a successful time on the computer instead of going away frustrated. Increase the font size—and consider making some oversized monitors available. Bigger sometimes really is better.

Speaking of bigger, another aid to emailers with low vision is the MAGic computer screen-magnification software, from Freedom Scientific (800-444-4443; http://www.freedomscientific.com).

The above are just a few of the tools available to handicapped computer users. The technology on this front is moving ahead rapidly, to the point that no one need be denied computer use because of physical constraints. The financial costs entailed may be a problem, both for individual users and for libraries and other institutions with limited budgets.

4. How Is Email Like Regular Mail?

In some ways, email resembles conventional mail. Anyone can imagine roughly what happens to an envelope containing a letter to your Uncle Fred that you drop into the U.S. mailbox on the corner. At some point, a postal carrier stops to empty the box. Your letter goes into a big bag with all the rest of the box's contents; postal workers sort the lot at a post office, send it off in different directions—and eventually, another postal carrier drops the letter into Uncle Fred's mailbox. Your letter might arrive two days after you mail it, or a week later. Or longer, by which time the exciting news you reported in the letter may have gone a tad stale.

Email works something like that, only a lot faster. When you click the Send button on your email, the system you use sends your message to Uncle Fred to a server. When your Uncle Fred logs on to a computer through his ISP, his ISP's server acts like a delivery vehicle, zipping the message relayed from your ISP's server to your Uncle Fred's email system. There is something like rocket science involved here, but, again, you don't need to know rocket science to send an email.

What About the Email Address?

If, as I have done, you try to send an email with an incomplete address, it will bounce back to you (usually quickly) as undeliverable. An email address has three parts, as in the address below:

rumplestiltskin@fairytales.com

The first part of the address is the user name. You will pick your own user name on most email systems. The second part of the address, following the "at" symbol (@), is the domain. The domain is, basically, the Internet service provider that handles your email in its server. The last part of the address is the "extension," which shows, more or less, to what kind of outfit the ISP belongs. Here are some domains:

.aero (air transport)
.com (commercial organizations; e.g., microsoft.com)
.coop (cooperatives)
.edu (higher education; e.g., umich.edu)
.net (networking organizations)
.gov (U.S. government entities; e.g., nasa.gov)
.mil (military entities; e.g., uscg.mil)
.museum (take a wild guess!)
.org (a grab-bag organizational domain)
.us (small business, local government, k-12 education)

Email systems are picky, picky, picky about addresses. Unlike your friendly and alert postal worker, no email program is going to make an educated guess that when you wrote "southave," you meant "southst." Omit a part of the email address, or make the teeniest of typos in it, and your email system will pick it up by two fingers with a sneer on its lip and drop it back in your inbox like a fish left lying out in the sun. You may have to study that address very closely to find the error in it.

What Makes a Good Password?

You will pick your own password to log on to the computer network and to your email program. Making good choices here can be more challenging than you might think. You'll want a password that is easy to remember, but that will be difficult for someone else to guess. Do your best to avoid obvious passwords, such as the names of your pets, your spouse, your children, your present street address or phone number, your birthday, or some other word or term that someone with a little knowledge about you might be able to discover with a little work. The most secure passwords are random combinations of letters and numbers, something like R493X52. There isn't much sentimental value in such a string of characters, but it will be very hard for anyone else to guess what it is.

An amusing little article in *Psychology Today* ("Passwords Reveal Your Personality," Jan./Feb. 2002) reports British psychologist Helen Petrie's findings on how people select their computer passwords. She identified four password genres, including "family-oriented" (the pet-name and birthday people); "fans" (who favor celebrity names—Madonna and Homer Simpson are popular); "fantasists," who like to think of themselves as "sexy" or "goddess"; and "cryptics." The cryptics were the smallest bunch in the group Petrie surveyed, a mere 10 percent—but their passwords are the most secure, like that random number-letter combination above. Lean toward joining the cryptic crew when you select a password. It won't be as much fun to type it into the computer as "loverguy" or "Fluffycat," but it will be much more secure.

5. Is "Email Privacy" an Oxymoron?

Speaking of security, Email lacks the inherent privacy of conventional mail. Although it is most unlikely that anyone working for your ISP would have the time, interest, or disregard for employment security required to dip into your email messages (think postal carrier and big bag of U.S. mail), what happens to your email after you send it is beyond your control. Your emails can be forwarded, deliberately or accidentally, to large numbers of people. They can hang around in both online and offline files for days, months, even years, where you can't touch them. When you send an email, you really don't know where it's going to end up. Because of its easily compromised security, it is wise to take some precautions with email. As mentioned earlier, institutional email systems are subject to surveillance; no one sending a private email on the company system should assume that a company official will not read it. As noted in *U.S. News & World Report* (July 24, 2000), an American Management Association Survey revealed that two-thirds of large American companies monitor employee email.

The Never, Ever List of Email Security Don'ts

• Never include critical account numbers in an email message. Do not send credit card numbers, checking or savings account numbers, or other numbers that in malicious hands could jeopardize the safety of your funds or that of others, or in some other way compromise your well being if used with ill intent.

• Never include your Social Security number in an email. Identity theft is a booming industry on the Internet, and nothing makes it easier for a felon in this game than loose Social Security numbers.

• Never send personal passwords (ATM, email, etc.) in an email. No reputable organization *ever* asks for passwords via email.

6. Etiquette: Making Emailing a Pleasant Experience

As several generations of writers on etiquette, and the entire population of Minnesota, have observed, it's nice to be nice. There are a number of things you can do with your email to make it agreeable to your recipients. Here are some:

Salutations

Use them. When you write a letter, you don't immediately begin your verbiage in the upper-left corner of the page. You include a salutation of some sort: "Dear Sir or Madam," "Dear John," or "Dear Sweetie," or something along those lines. Follow the same practice with email. Leaping immediately into the message, unless the message is one in a series being exchanged in rapid sequence, so that it's like part of a running conversation, is either not friendly (if you're writing to a friend), or unbusinesslike (if you're writing to an organization, or to a person with whom you are not personally acquainted).

You can use much the same sorts of salutations in email as in conventional mail: Dear Editors; Dear Friends; Dear Acme Dynamite Company; or, in a pinch, when you are not at all sure to whom you email is going in an organization (it happens), simply "Hello...." A friend and I who have been exchanging emails for years address each other by initial: "Hi, C." "Hi, G." The salutation depends, as so much does, on the circumstances. Use one, though. Your email will make a better impression if you do.

Emailing to Strangers

If you're writing to someone who does not know you—our explosive friends at the Acme Dynamite Co., let's say—approach your email the way you would any conventional business letter. Include a reasonably formal salutation, identify yourself, succinctly state your business, thank the recipient for his or her time, and close with an appropriate line, such as "I look forward to hearing from you," if, in fact, you do. Don't go on and on about your topic, however unsatisfying that last shipment from Acme may have been. Get in, state your case, and get out before your message grows tedious. Chances are good that your email recipient has lots of email to read. A brief message from you will be so pleasant, in contrast to the verbose missives that clutter the company in-box.

Emailing to the People We Know: Let's Get Personal

Many have written on email regarding its "impersonal" nature. Because it is "impersonal," they say, because it does not convey tone of voice

or emotions as well as face-to-face conversation or even a telephone conversation, one should steer clear of emails freighted with emotional or other
significant personal content, or, if one indulges in such content, might do
well to assist the reader in its apprehension through the use of smileys.
(More on those irritating critters later.)

Excuse me, but: Baloney. There is no reason why a carefully written
email cannot be as clearly expressive of emotional and personal content as
a clearly-written letter, and there is no reason to send emails that are not
clearly written. The speed with which emails travel to their destinations is
not an excuse for slovenly composition, or for patronizing intelligent readers with silly typographical tricks to "help" them understand what you
mean to say. Do you draw smiley or frowny faces at the ends of your sentences in letters? Then why on earth would you draw them in an email?

Some who have written on email are cautious about the medium to
the point, perhaps, of low-grade obsession, advising us never to send an
email that we wouldn't mind seeing printed in the local paper. This advice
seems to me suggestive of an email reticence that guts much of the plea-
sure from correspondence with those one trusts. Now, the circumstances
are different within a corporate or other institutional email system, in
which emails do not "belong" to their senders. Managers do have a legal
right of surveillance over employee email. Email may also be archived in
corporate files, so today's blunder could prove next year's embarrassment.
Today's blunder can also be today's embarrassment, given a careless forwarding of a sensitive message ("Don't you think our new boss is a petty
tyrant?").

But if you're sending an email to your trusted Uncle Fred from your
home computer or the public library workstation, don't you want the freedom to be able say, e.g., that you think your neighbor's 18-year-old kid is
a complete nitwit who should be closely guarded for his own safety? You
probably wouldn't want that opinion plastered across the front page of
your hometown paper, but what are the chances of Uncle Fred's being
indiscreet enough to relay your message in that direction? Furthermore,
what fun is correspondence if you can't let your hair down for fear of public revelation of the snarls? Not much.

In view of human nature and habits of communication, it is unreal-
istic to expect or advise people to play the Goody Twoshoes role, or, failing
goodness, that of the paranoid retentive, every time they sit down at the
keyboard to send an email. People send emails from the complete range of
emotion: elated, sad, angry, depressed, cheerful, puzzled. Email, like conventional mail, issues from the full spectrum of the emotional rainbow, and

one would not want to see it any other way. The fundamental desire for freedom, spontaneity, and candor in personal communication knocks tight-lipped rules of discretion into the wastebasket.

Remember, though: Judge your emails by the circumstances. Consider whether what you are writing is appropriate and acceptable for the situation. Think of how you might feel about the content of your email a week from now, when the mood of the moment has passed. Will you still find it truthful? Humane? Thoughtfully composed? If not, you may want to rethink sending it. Over the centuries, countless conventional letters have been written and mailed at white emotional heat, only to leave their authors ruing at length their intemperate correspondence. Such letters have inflicted much pointless pain, and many of their writers would give nearly anything to have them back, and unread. Because email is so much faster a medium than the conventional letter, it is even easier to commit a gross faux pas with it. If the message you just composed has any content that might rile the receiver, heed the words of the old Brook Benton song: Think twice. Think it over before you click the Send button.

Email's Big Advantage

Email, in fact, has one incalculable advantage over both telephone and face-to-face communication: You can think a long time between and during sentences. If you utter a sentence that you don't like, you can go back and rewrite it. You can (and should) go back and reread your entire message, to be sure that it says what you mean to say, as clearly as you can say it. Thanks to its very freedom from the tone of the spoken word, email can help take the edge off some exchanges that might otherwise run aground in raised voices and exasperated, inarticulate arguments. I am not the only one who has often found email with late-adolescent children an island of calm communication over difficult topics that might not have gone so well in person or in a telephone conversation.

But You'd Better Not Shout

So yes, if you feel the need to broach emotional or personal topics in your email, go ahead. Exercise some discretion. DO NOT, NO MATTER HOW MUCH ADRENALINE IS RUNNING THROUGH YOUR VEINS, LOCK DOWN YOUR CAPS KEY AND DO THIS through the entire length of an email. Experienced emailers refer to this tactic as "shouting." It is the email equivalent of walking into your coworker's office and pounding your fist on the table while you bellow your objections to the company line. It is uncouth. It makes your email hard to read, and many people—including me—won't bother to read it at all. Just—don't, OK? If you refrain from this unfortunate habit, you will be doing your part to spread peace and light in the online world.

Subject Lines

Every email program includes a subject line in the message screen. This is where you alert your message recipient to the content of the email. Use a subject line that has some clearly discernible connection to the message. Remember, the first place your recipients obtain a clue regarding your messages' content will be in the list of messages in their inbox. A blank subject line is utterly useless, as well as lazy and a little insulting. A subject line with no direct bearing on the content of the message is also worthless.

Watch Your Spelling, Punctuation, and Capitalization

Email is usually a more relaxed medium than conventional letters or memos, but "relaxed" does not mean "flaccid." Everyone makes an occasional goof, but few readers enjoy receiving email with wantonly butchered spelling, eccentric or absent capitalization (leave the first-person singular "i" to e.e. cummings, if you would), or grammar that staggers across the screen like a buffalo broadsided by a stagecoach. Aside from making messages hard, and sometimes impossible, to understand, such carelessness suggests to your email recipients that you don't consider them important enough to bother tending to the niceties. Do give these niceties some attention. You'll seem ever so much brighter and more considerate in your readers' eyes, not to mention enhancing the likelihood that your recipients will take the time to read what you send them. As a newspaper editor told me (speaking generally, because I *do* use the shift key): "If you're too lazy to use the shift key, I don't want to hear from you." Use the shift key. Many email programs include automatic spell checkers to help you out. Use them, too!

After You Write It, Edit It

Spelling, capitalization, and grammar are part of this. The other part rests chiefly on getting to your point, making it in a polite, concise (and, when appropriate, entertaining) fashion, and saying good-bye. We have all known people who could almost literally bore us to tears with their rambling, endless, self-centered monologs. It is entirely possible to take the same approach in email, and many do. A major difference is that while someone trapped in a face-to-face "conversation" with an egotistical bore might be too polite to turn and walk away, the email recipient of a message that advances on such a front might decide quickly to close it up, and even delete it, rather than endure its pointless loquaciousness to the last numbing sentence.

Even in chatty email, one can be focused and economical. Aim for that effect. Again, your email correspondents will look forward to your messages if you show some consideration for their sensibilities.

Forwarding: Do You or Don't You?

Most email programs make it very easy to forward messages to others that you receive from a given sender. Forwarding emails is much like taking a letter someone has written to you, stuffing it into an envelope, and mailing it to a third party, with or without your own comments. The inherent dangers of such behavior are obvious. They are so obvious that some people who have written on email believe that one should never forward an email without asking permission of the sender.

That position strikes me as both logistically cumbersome and needlessly sensitive. Many emails, both in the business and personal spheres, are so innocuous in their presentation of matter-of-fact, impersonal information that asking permission to forward them is simply finicky. Suppose your good friend George emails you the manufacturer's service recommendations for the snowblower you purchased from him. Your cousin in Duluth has the same kind of snowblower. Is there some good reason for you not to forward those recommendations to your cousin without asking George's permission? It strains credibility to think so. It would be polite to let your cousin know that you are passing this information on thanks to George's assistance, but that should be sufficient.

On the other hand, suppose George emails you a message describing his family's grief at the death of their beloved cocker spaniel. You have another friend who recently lost a dear animal companion, and you believe that George's touching, heartfelt message would help your friend contend with her own loss. What do you do?

If you have any regard for George's feelings and privacy, you ask him if it's OK with him if you forward his message, after explaining why you would like to do so. His message, after all, was a deeply personal one in which he revealed not the lubrication requirements for a two-cycle engine, but the inner places of his heart. That is not the kind of message you forward to anyone else without obtaining its sender's go-ahead.

The etiquette of forwarding messages depends, like almost every other aspect of social intercourse, on the specifics of the situation. What works in one set of circumstances is inappropriate or worse—perhaps far worse—in another. Take your time. Think it through before you click the Send button. Once you have made that click, you want to sit back in comfort with yourself. You do not want to second guess yourself about whether you should have sent the message. I know: I have been sending email for a long time, and I have zipped off a few that, after sending, I asked myself "Was that such a good idea?" That is not the sort of thought you want following you around during the day.

Sending Copies of Emails

Whatever email program you decide to use (and you may use more than one) will offer you the option of sending copies of your messages to people other than the primary recipients whose addresses you enter in the "To:" field. As a rule, you will have two choices for copies: "Cc" ("carbon copy") and "Bcc" (blind carbon copy). These terms are holdovers from earlier office days: There is no carbon in these copies! There could be trouble ahead, however, if you do not show some discretion in your copying.

Do you know for a fact that people whose addresses you list in the Cc field don't mind having their addresses thus broadcast? Some email users are very cautious with their addresses; they don't want the world at large, or even the local neighborhood, to know how to reach them by email. Casual inclusion of email addresses in the Cc field might violate the privacy walls that one of the copied recipients has been working hard to maintain.

That leaves the Bcc field. This is a touchy area. When you send a blind copy, the primary recipient is unaware that such a copy has gone out. There are times when tact and sensitivity call for a blind copy, but using this function too often can give an emailer the reputation of someone who, in effect, talks behind people's backs. That is a tough reputation to overcome. One way around it: When you send a message that you want to copy to people, address the message to yourself (yes, you can send emails to yourself), and include all the people to whom you would like to send copies in the Bcc field. This approach shows all recipients that you are protecting their privacy, at the same time as not hiding from the primary recipient (yourself!) the identities of people to whom you are sending copies.

Oh, this tangled Web we weave... speaking of which:

Sending Web Links

With many email programs you can include in your messages links ("hyperlinks") to Web sites. Your recipients can click on the links and go to the sites through their browsers. This is a nice capability. If you send a link, take care to include the complete URL (Uniform Resource Locator), from "http:" on through to the end. The smallest missing detail or typo in a URL will render it inoperable. Before I send any Web link in an email, I click on the link I have typed to see if it works. I have discovered a lot of typos this way. This double-check takes but a few seconds, and can spare your message recipients the task of a response to your message that goes something like this: "Hi, John. That URL you sent me doesn't work. Want to try again?"

How to End an Email

Just as it is more civil to open an email with a salutation of some sort, even if it's something as casual as "Hi, Joe!" careful emailers will finish their messages with something resembling a signature. Email signatures are not graced by the idiosyncratic penmanship of a name signed by hand at the end of a letter, but the absence of some closing "sign-off" gives a message the effect of an audio tape snipped off in mid-passage. The impression is one of abruptness, and not a little rudeness, intended or not.

Some people construct elaborate email signatures, with their names all but lost in typographical artwork that bears some relation to their interests or occupations. Smileys are but the crude beginnings of the amazing decorative effects email users can achieve with the characters on a standard computer keyboard. Most email programs make it easy to save these creations and apply them automatically to one's outgoing mail. The temptation to run amuck with Byzantine signatures is strong, especially for creative people new to email.

Want some advice from this jaded emailer? Sure, you do. Keep your signature simple. Forget the artwork. That's not why people open your emails. ("Oh, boy! Frank just sent me another email with his 48-line signature depicting a statue of Buddha with a clock in his stomach!") Your name, organizational affiliation and title (if this is business correspondence), address, and phone number are sufficient. If you have a personal or business Web page, it's usually acceptable to include your page's URL. Everything other than these details is probably better left on the shelf, and sometimes much of what I just mentioned here belongs there, too. How helpful is it to send a close friend email after email with your address and phone number, as though it were fresh news? Your friends know you, and how to reach you. For such emails, a quick sign-off is fine:

Take care! –Max
Talk to you later! –Jane
Cheers—Bill

For people with whom you exchange email frequently, several times a week or more, and who know you well, less is more in the way of signatures. Most of my emails to my boss, with whom I have been working closely for a decade, end this simply:

Thanks. –G.

My boss knows who "G" is. If he doesn't, it's too late for me to try to tell him.

They Won't Believe You Read the Whole Thing!

Not if you didn't, they won't. Do not reply to email messages that you have not read from start to finish. If you reply before you finish reading, you will rapidly drive your correspondents nuts. I guarantee it. You will neglect to answer questions that they ask; you will misinterpret their messages; you will waste their time by forcing them to send you fresh messages in which they must restate what they told you in the first place, or find some gentle way to correct your misimpressions. After a few such occasions you might see a reply like this: "Will you please read the &*#* message?!" Except your correspondent probably wouldn't use those substitute characters for, ah, vigorous language. Worst of all, if you jump the gun on your email replies, you will make yourself look like an idiot. We all look that way at times, but there is no need to achieve the condition by "answering" an email that you have not fully read. Sometimes the most important part of an email is the last sentence or phrase. Don't stop reading until you have finished it. Please.

Take Your Time in Composition

One of my favorite episodes in the old *Twilight Zone* series, "A Stop at Willoughby," concerned an executive who worked in a high-pressure job. His tyrannical boss liked to remind him that "It's a push-push-push business!" Isn't it, though? The world has speeded up; everything happens in an instant: coffee, potatoes, stock reports, television news, wars, and email. Attention spans seem to shrink weekly. The pressure to provide product Right Away, ASAP, is powerful, and our society indoctrinates us with the notion that if we slow down and take our time, we're headed for the ash heap.

We may all be headed for the ash heap anyhow, but why rush to get there? When you compose an email, think through what you're saying. Try to be gentle, informative, friendly, businesslike, reflective—or any combination of those qualities, as the situation warrants. Hasty messages tend to be poor messages. (As usual, I know: I've sent them!)

Sometimes you may find it necessary to compose a particularly difficult message, perhaps to a friend, a relative, or a business associate. Such messages demand close attention. They often involve emotional baggage. The "Draft" folder, available in most email programs, was made for such messages. Write your message, save it in the Draft folder, let it sit a spell, then go back and reread it. You'll probably find ways to make it better. If there is no draft folder in the program you use, you can simply send the message to yourself, open it later and rework it, then forward it to your intended recipient.

Timely Replies

You are not obligated to reply to all your email, any more than you are required to answer your front door every time someone knocks. Even if you use an email program that screens for junk mail, you will, from time to time, see the occasional message that you know you can delete without even opening ("Make Big $$ Working at Home!!"), much less replying to.

Most of your messages, though, will probably come from people who either know you personally or have some good reason to send you a message. It will be most agreeable to them if you respond to their messages within a reasonable time. That doesn't always mean "right away." It doesn't even mean "today," as a rule. It means, rather, that you reply while the message is reasonably fresh. Email is a little like baked goods. Day-old donuts are still tasty. If they have sat around for a week, they might be better used as paperweights, the grease spots notwithstanding.

Responding to today's email tomorrow is usually OK. Day after tomorrow will probably work. Sometimes later than that will do, too. But keep in mind one of the major assets of email: its currency. Letting email that deserves replies languish in your in-box for more than a few days achieves the electronic equivalent of those very stale donuts, and defeats the inherent virtue of email's ability to overcome the barriers of time that obstruct conventional mail. Even if you don't have time at the moment for a thorough reply, those who send you messages and hope for responses will appreciate a quick holding action on your part—a message that says something like "Thanks, got your message; will reply at length later!"

Attachments: Can Your Recipient Open Them?

One of the delights (and dangers) of email is that it makes it easy to send already-existing files to others with your messages. You can send documents, spreadsheets, pictures, music and video clips—just about anything that will fit into the space your email program allows you to use. The dangers of computer viruses are real and serious. I'll return to them in the sections on separate email systems, but there is one etiquette matter to tend here.

Let's say that you are eager to send as an email attachment a photo of your charming new grandchild (or puppy, kitten, backyard deck, lawn mower, whatever) to your friend in another state. Does your friend have a program that will permit viewing the photo? You and your email recipients open attachments with programs on your computers *other than* your email programs. If you don't know for sure that your friend has a program able to handle your attachment, ask before you send it. For that matter, some email programs simply don't support attachments. You may find that it will serve your friend's needs better if you pop a picture of that precious kitty into the U.S. Mail.

7. Pass on Passing the Spam: Unwelcome Commercial Solicitations, Chain Letters, and Other Annoying, Often Illegal, and Occasionally Obscene Email Drivel

Spam is to email that you want to receive what a telemarketing call is to phone calls that you want to answer. Picture yourself at the end of the day, having just sat down to supper after a tough one at the office or around the house. All you want to do is to relax, have a quiet meal, maybe chat a bit with your spouse or significant other. The phone rings. You leap up, thinking it might be one of the kids. But no. There's a faraway pause after you say hello, and the caller finally says, "Hello, Mr. Jones. How are you this evening?"

You were better before you answered the phone. If you're not bold enough to hang up immediately, you will hear at least the beginning of a fast, grating sales pitch for a product or service you wouldn't buy from these people in 12 lifetimes. If you decline politely, the caller may (to your amazement—it has happened to me!) attempt to pick an argument with you about why you don't want it.

That's what spam and other junk email are like. It's more than a little unfair to Hormel, the manufacturer of Spam luncheon meat, that its product's name has been appropriated and lower-cased to denote one of the most irritating presences on the Internet. I've eaten Spam. It's not bad at all, especially with scrambled eggs. Furthermore, Hormel recently established in Austin, Minnesota, a 16,500 square foot museum dedicated to Spam—the only lunch meat with its own museum! But spam is bad, and the more email you do, spreading your email address out there on the big old Internet where con artists and cheap operators can find it, the more likely it is that you will find spam in your in-box, along with chain letters, hoaxes, and appeals to purchase Web access to "xxx nude Lutheran choir members!" Although a growing number of states have enacted anti-spam legislation, emailers living in those states are not immune from seeing spam in their message lists.

How Do You Know It's Spam?

If you receive an email from a person or organization that you have never heard of promising you incredible rewards for little or nothing, that's spam. If you see a string of exclamation points in the subject line, you're probably looking at spam. (Spammers know their way around the Internet, but they tend to know zilch about effective advertising, and believe that a string of exclamation points will get you excited and lead you to hand over your credit card number!!!!) Another tip-off that you have received spam is a return email address that consists of numbers, for example, *489723@suckers.com.*

According to Michael A. Covington in his article "Ethics and the Internet" (*Electronics Now*, Sept. 1997), spam made its debut in April of 1994, when a pair of Arizona lawyers posted an advertisement for their services to immigrants on some 8,000 newsgroups. Global outrage ensued, but the spam-masters simply cranked up their skills. Today, sophisticated spammers use fake addresses, fake names, foreign domains (Chile and Korea are popular), and other slippery tactics to keep grinding out their unethical tripe.

Yes, alas. The Internet is clogged with email so fundamentally dumb, dishonest, witlessly credulous, and plain downright nasty that it has no excuse for existence, aside from its connection with one or more of the Seven Deadly Sins. You will not be an emailer for long before you find it in your in-box, often in spite of the best efforts of your email program to block it. You will see the glorious, unsolicited commercial pitches of spam, for products of dubious and nonexistent merit; you will see heartbreaking chain letters promising that if you send a dozen copies of this email to your friends, the American Cancer Society will contribute five cents toward a cure for Little Jimmy's tragic condition. You will see messages promising that you can "Make Money Fast" if you will only blah, blah, blah... You will see frenetic warnings about deadly computer viruses.

Junk, Junk, Junk!

This stuff is all junk. Well-meaning, guileless people spread much of it around the Internet, believing that they really are helping the Little Jimmies of the world, or helping to save civilization from horrid computer viruses. Sometimes—chiefly the "Make Big Bucks" crowd—the motivation is pure greed and a desire to exploit others through con games, usually the electronic equivalent of the universally-illegal pyramid scheme. Sometimes the motivation lies in an ambition to take advantage of public anxiety about computer crime. Many scurrilous hoaxsters have spread disinformation, if not panic, in email regarding "new viruses." You may receive a message like this from an unknown party, or forwarded in wide-eyed good faith, by a friend:

From: cassandra@panicinthestreets.net
To: My Closest 500 Friends
Subject: CNN Announces Killer Computer Virus!
Early this morning, CNN announced a new computer virus, the Asian Warthog Virus, which has no known cure. It comes in an email with the subject line "Ima Warthog." If you open it, the message will activate a virus that destroys your hard drive, sends itself to all the people in your address book, eats all the food in your refrigerator, and sells your dog to a vivisectionist. The

ONLY WAY to stop this virus is to send this message to EVERYONE YOU KNOW ASAP. Officials at both IBM and AOL have reported massive breakdowns in their corporate computing systems because of the Warthog virus. Please, whatever you do, forward this message to everyone you know RIGHT NOW! THIS IS NOT A HOAX!

The above "message" only slightly exaggerates some of the ludicrous virus hoax emails that I have seen. They commonly refer to some respected organizations with ties to high technology—CNN, AOL, IBM, Microsoft—to give their panic mongering a flavor of credibility. As soon as you see the claim that "This is not a hoax," you know immediately that this message is, in fact, a hoax. Do not forward these messages to anyone. Aside from wasting people's time, they can, if forwarded in sufficient numbers (we're talking millions of forwardings here), clog the Internet like a greaseball in the kitchen drain. That's the objective of the cranks who originate them. What cards, eh? Do not forward these messages to anyone. Read them if you wish, laugh a bitter laugh at human folly, and delete them.

If you would like to look further into Internet hoaxes and scams, there are a number of good sites on the Web. I like the one that the Symantec Corporation operates: *http://www.symantec.com/avcenter/hoax.html*

When You Receive Spam, Chain Letters, and Other Junk Email

• *Never respond to it.* A favorite ploy of spammers (who in another life would be wearing yellow plaid sport coats and selling used cars with shot transmissions to widows and orphans) is to include a line in a come-on telling the recipient to send a message to such-and-such an address to be removed from the mailing list. ***Don't do it!*** By responding to that message, you will be confirming to this Internet lowlife that your email address is a good one, and you will receive still more irritating, worthless mail. Oh, the humanity! Keep in mind that the easiest way to get out of a con game is not to get into it.

• *Never forward chain letters.* They are the work of sadists and confidence men (and women) playing on the sentiments and fears of the gullible, and they chew up vast reams of computer space. You will *not* "make big $$$" by forwarding chain email, or by following instructions therein on where to send money; you will *not* contribute to a cure for Little Jimmy's terminal case of hangnails; you will *not* win a free vacation. If you succumb to this stuff, you *will* get ripped off, if in no other way than through your time being wasted. Time is a precious commodity that becomes more so with every day that passes; don't let these Internet con artists steal any of yours.

The Forwarder's 12 Step Program

A friend of mine forwarded me (what else?) the following parody of serious 12-step programs. I cannot locate the original Internet source, but trust that the author will not mind my repeating it here, both for the laughs and for the good sense behind them:

1. I will *not* get bad luck, lose my friends, or lose my mailing lists if I don't forward an email!

2. I will *not* hear any music or see a taco dog if I do forward an email.

3. Bill Gates is *not* going to send me money, and Victoria's Secret doesn't know anything about a gift certificate they're supposed to send me if I forward an email.

4. Ford will *not* give me a 50 percent discount even if I forward an email to more than 50 people.

5. I will *never* receive gift certificates, coupons, or freebies from Coca-Cola, Cracker Barrel, Old Navy, or anyone else if I send an email to 10 people.

6. I will *never* see a pop-up window if I forward an email…never, ever!

7. There is *no such thing* as an email tracking program, and I am not stupid enough to think that someone will send me $100 for forwarding an email to 10 or more people!

8. There is *no* kid with cancer in England collecting anything through the Make-a-Wish program. He did when he was seven years old. He is now cancer-free and 35 years old and doesn't want any more postcards or get-well cards.

9. The government does *not* have a bill in Congress called 901B (or whatever they named it this week) that, if passed, will enable them to charge us five cents for every email we send.

10. There will be *no* cool dancing, singing, waving, colorful flowers, characters, or program that I will receive immediately after I forward an email. None, zip, zero, nada!

11. The American Red Cross will *not* donate 50 cents to certain individuals dying of some never-heard-of disease for every email address to which I forward a message. The American Red Cross receives donations.

12. And finally, I will *not* let others guilt me into forwarding messages by telling me if I don't forward them, I am not their friend or that I don't believe in Jesus Christ. If God wants to send me a message, I believe the bushes in my yard will burn before He picks up a PC to pass it on!

If you are really, really irritated over a given piece of junk email or spam, rather than trying to send an indignant reply to the source of the message—please, don't waste your time—contact your ISP and let the folks there know what has happened. Your ISP managers can probably take some constructive action if they become aware of a virulent email offender. No conscientious ISP wants to be a medium for spamming, and most will cancel the account of anyone who violates the ISP's standards.

Some Other Spam Avoidance Tips

Writing in the *Los Angeles Times* (Nov. 8, 2001), Lawrence J. Magid made a number of useful points:

• Do not post your email address in public places.
• Take care about sending your email address; if you're dealing with a mailing list or a Web site in which you are not confident, use a secondary mail system. For example, if you do your serious emailing through Outlook, approach perhaps-dubious sources through an alternate, like Yahoo! Mail. If the spam starts flying, it will not gum up your primary mail system.
• Avoid posting your email address on a Web site or on a newsgroup.
• If you use AOL chat rooms, employ a separate screen name.

8. A Few Words on Our Common Enemies, the Viruses

Getting back to those real and serious dangers (you might, speaking casually, say that they are "real serious" dangers) of computer viruses, there are certain measures that every wise computer user observes. Email attachments are the favorite mode of transmission for these viruses. If you want to join the wise user group, you will equip your computer with an antivirus program, and use it to scan incoming attachments if your mail program does not perform this function automatically. These programs are, as a rule, inexpensive compared to the amount you laid out for your computer and peripherals; you should be able to find a good antivirus program for well under $50. Making that initial investment may entitle you to complimentary updates from the vendor.

As indicated above, some free email programs do include virus-checking functions. Good for them! Whatever program you use, do not consider opening an attachment unless you are confident that it is virus-free. Even trusted sources (best friends, your boss, your boss's boss) can inadvertently send attachments containing viruses. Viruses can be such a headache if turned loose in your computer that, when looking at a message with an attachment that you really want to open, right now, without ascertaining its bug-free status, you should not be tempted, not even once. You should not say, "Oh, this attachment is from Uncle Fred, and he's been my favorite uncle forever. What could it hurt to look just this once without checking for a virus?"

It could hurt a lot. It could cost you big bucks down at the local computer doctor's office, and it could do evil things to data you have stored in your hard drive. Stifle the impulse to open that attachment in a state of naïve faith.

Admittedly, I'm a little touchy on this topic. That touchiness comes from my experience battling a computer virus that would not die over a period of several months, back in the days when I was not as careful about attachments as I am now. Every time I thought I had the bug eradicated from my machine, it crawled out of some hidden cranny and started chewing on my documents again. I finally took the step of last resort: I backed up all my files (which I should have been doing routinely, of course), and had everything, including all my programs, wiped clean from the hard drive. Then I had to reinstall it all. Fun! And such an entertaining expense of a couple of days' time!

In his worthwhile article "Tame Your In-Box" (*PC World*, June 2001), Steve Bass suggests a number of useful tips on taking charge of one's email. He refers to attachments as "potential virus bombs," and emphasizes his "Rule Numero Uno: Always save attachments to your hard drive and scan them with an antivirus tool before you view them."

Woody Leonhard is the guiding light behind the Web site *Woody's Office Watch* (*http://www.woodyswatch.com*). Mr. Leonhard offers much useful advice on his site, which is especially worth a visit for anyone who uses Microsoft operating systems and other Microsoft products. His counsel on email attachments leaves no wiggle room, and goes one step beyond Bass's Rule: "Don't ever open (or run) a file attached to an email message until you contact the person who sent you the message and make sure it's OK.

Once you get the go-ahead, manually run the attachment through your antivirus software before you open it, just for good measure."

In other words, trust no one. This email business sounds more like television's *The X-Files* every step of the way, doesn't it?

I'm not quite as sensitive as Mr. Leonhard about attachments; I'll trust my antivirus program, and probably not call people who sent me attachments to nag them about their electronic cleanliness. A rational middle ground between raving paranoia and dewy innocence will probably work for most people. It's worth remembering, too, that most email messages do not come with attachments. They're the exception, not the rule, so don't lose sleep over them, or refuse to connect your computer to the Internet for fear that some wicked virus will have its way with your hard drive. If you practice safe computing—all the time, not just most of the time—it probably won't. (Note that I said "probably." There are no guarantees here, friends.)

9. Smileys, Acronyms, and Initialisms

My distaste for smileys has probably come through clearly by this point. I feel the same way about initialisms intended to stand in for honest, real words and comprehensibly expressed ideas. However I feel about these little pests, millions of emailers are devoted to them. Millions of people watch "reality TV," too. Don't blame me! But ignore my wrinkled-up nose when I get near these things. I would not be doing my duty if I hid from you, the beginning emailer, the lexicon of symbols and initialisms that our brother and sister emailers so generally find so irresistible. You may find them irresistible, too. That's all right with me, as long as you let me grump off into the sunset without using them. If you want to use them, fire away.

Smileys (Also known as emoticons—"emotional icons")

You bang out these little typographical doohickeys using punctuation marks and occasional letters on your keyboard. Here's a bunch; there are undoubtedly countless others in the Beta testing stage. If you're hungry for more, invent your own—or use any Web search engine on the term "emoticons." You'll be deluged. By the way (excuse me; I mean BTW), you have to look at these things sideways to get the point.

:) Grin	:-] Amused irony
:-) Grin with nose	:-[Morose irony
: (Sad	:-< Terribly distressed
:- (Sad with nose	:-# Lips are sealed
;-) Wink	:-} Goofy grin
:-> Satanic leer	:-1 Smirk
:-D Laughing	:-\ Undecided
:-O Shouting	>:-< Really peeved
:-P Tongue hanging out	0:-) Angelic
:-P~~ Tongue hanging out	}:> Devilish
and drooling	:'-(Crying

Isn't that fun? If you must use these things, try to go easy on them. A touch of salt on a fried egg makes it tastier; too much salt buries the flavor and makes the whole business unpalatable. It works the same way with emails and smileys.

Acronyms and Initialisms

Acronyms (words formed from combining the first letters of the words in a name or phrase) and initialisms (the same sort of combination, but not resulting in a pronounceable word) purportedly save time in composition and create a tighter, more concise message. IMNSHO, what they do better is to encourage a clubby, in-group atmosphere among emailers, while at the same time relieving people of having to reflect on what they really mean to say. The computing world is already adequately overstuffed with in-group elitism, but as the motorcycle aficionados' motto goes, "Let those who ride decide." Do what you will with these substitutes for plain speaking. If you want more, search "email acronyms" on the Web. You'll find more than you can stand.

AFAIK (As far as I know)
AKA (Also known as)
BTW (By the way)
FAQ (Frequently asked questions)
F2F (Face to face)
FWIW (For what it's worth)
FYI (For your information)
GMTA (Great minds think alike)
HAND (Have a nice day)

HHOK (Ha ha only kidding)
IAC (In any case)
IANAL (I am not a lawyer [but…])
ICCL (I couldn't care less)
IMO (In my opinion)
IMHO (In my humble opinion)
IMNSHO (In my not so humble opinion)
IRL (In real life)
J/K (Just kidding)
LABATYD (Life's a bitch and then you die)
LOL (Laughing out loud)
LTNS (Long time no see)
NP (No problem)
OTOH (On the other hand)
PLS (Please)
ROTFL (Rolling on the floor laughing)
RSN (Real soon now)
RTM (Read the manual)
Thx (Thanks)
TTFN (Ta ta for now)
TNSTAAFL (There's no such thing as a free lunch)
WB (Welcome back)
WRT (With respect to)
WTG (Way to go)
YMMV (Your mileage may vary)
EA! (Enough already! [I just made up this one.])

10. Learn to Use Folders

Email programs generally make it possible to establish a variety of folders (sometimes called "mailboxes") in which you can organize your messages. Setting up a good roster of folders is an important step in email management. Without them, you will soon find it all but impossible to keep track of anything, coming or going. That good roster of folders, however, is only part of the job. The other duty in email management is to discipline yourself sufficiently that you routinely assign messages to your folders, rather than simply letting them languish in your inbox or sent mail folder. Some programs provide "filters" that allow you to send incoming mail automatically to specific folders. A nice feature!

I tend to get behind in my folder management, and sometimes, as a result, hold what I call "email days," or half-days, when I spend a lot more time than I want to spend going through my inbox and sent folder, rereading messages that I've forgotten, and either assigning them to appropriate folders, if they're keepers, or deleting them. It is faster and easier to tend to this business in a timely fashion. Perhaps you can be more diligent in this task than I have been!

11. *Minding the Ps and Qs of Formatting*

You might like to know that the term "Ps and Qs" quite likely originated as shorthand for "pints and quarts," having to do with the quantity of restorative beverages (generally of an alcoholic persuasion) that sailors were allotted in the old days. When my grade school teachers told me to mind my Ps and Qs, I thought they meant that literally. They probably did. Now, of course, the term refers generally to attention to details, not to a sailor's libations when he's off duty. Let's tend to some general email housekeeping details before we get into the systems themselves, specifically concerning formatting of email messages.

How Long to Make a Line

Different email programs do not always handle each other's messages with grace and aplomb. One of the most basic matters of email business is line length. It probably won't be long in your emailing career before you receive a message that, upon your opening it, spreads itself all over your screen in erratic, if not wholly irrational, lines. Your eyes will dance back and forth trying to make sense of the mess; if it's a long message, you may give up and reply to the sender with a puzzled inquiry.

The message did not look like that when it was sent. The problem lies in the imperfect ability of two email programs to "talk" to each other. It might help to think of the line-length and other formatting snags as reminiscent of traffic on American railroads before the standardized track gauge. In the pre-standard days, Engineer Jones could be rolling along with a good head of steam, but have to come to a dead stop at the end of his own company's track because a competing line's continuing track spaced the rails an inch closer together. Engineer Jones's train could not travel on them.

Different email systems, too, can have a hard time handling each other's freight. If you know that your recipient uses the same email program that you do, there should be no problem. You will often not know that, however. Sending your messages in plain text, not all gussied up with special formatting that might come through as mush in someone else's inbox, is one important way to minimize this problem. Another effective tactic to reduce formatting problems is to keep an eye on the length of your lines—and instead of relying on your email program's word wraparound feature (the program function that automatically moves your message to a new line when you have typed to the end of the present one), press the Enter key at the end of each line. You may find that the email program you come to rely on allows you to set a default line length in its system options. The Hotmail Web email program is one that offers this option.

Some email authorities recommend a good line length as about 65 characters, including spaces. The Enter key tactic helps retain a good paragraph format in email programs that do not respond to your program's word-wrap feature. Getting in the habit of using a 65-character line with the Enter key (it won't take long until you do this effortlessly) can sometimes make a huge difference in the readability of your emails. I have received emails with lines so haphazardly arranged, thanks to not-very compatible systems, that I could barely read them. The longer the message, the worse the ordeal for the reader in such a situation.

Shun the Tab Key

Avoid using the tab key when composing email. Use the space bar to indent. Pounding away at the space bar is a little more work, but the reason for it goes back to the analogy of the railroad tracks. Different email systems react to the tab indication in different ways. If you use the tab key to indent, what looks clean and pretty on your screen may look chaotic on your recipient's screen.

Making Long Messages More Readable

Many email messages—probably most—are no more than a paragraph long. If you go to multiple paragraphs, give your recipient a little more help by double spacing between paragraphs. That will improve readability. You might also consider applying the newspaper journalist's rule of thumb regarding paragraph length: If you're going past three or four sentences, start a new paragraph. Large blocks of unbroken print are hard on the eye in a newspaper, and on the printed page, too. They are even worse on a computer screen. Have mercy on your readers in this respect, and they will look forward to your emails.

Some writers on email counsel short messages as a general operational rule. Don't become overly concerned with what the "experts" think on this subject. Different circumstances call for different approaches. Certainly, most business correspondence, whether on paper or in email, should be concise. The story changes when you're corresponding with close friends; I have received many long emails from friends discussing issues of concern to them, and I have sent many such emails, too. If you feel like letting your hair down and your sentences roll on, roll away if the specifics of the situation make a long message suitable.

How Reply Formatting Helps You Keep Track

As a rule, when you send a reply to an email, the system will place a greater-than character (>) before each line of the original text that you leave in the message. If your email correspondent replies to your reply to his or her original message, the message will probably come back to you with double greater-than characters (>>) before lines from the original message, and single greater-than characters before lines from your original reply. Lengthy exchanges on the same topic can leave the message screen looking as though a thousand chickens have walked across it, but the greater-than markings do allow anyone to determine the chronological order of the content. Here is a simple example, with the messages in chronological order from the bottom up (I've omitted the usual extraneous stuff—signatures, headers, and what-not):

Jim,
OK w/me! By the way, how's the anger management course coming? ;-)—Bill

>Hi Bill,
>Sorry, I threw my new driver into the pond last week. You can
>Use my new putter, though. –Jim

>>Hi, Jim.
>>Sounds good to me! Can I use your new driver?—Bill

>>>Hi, Bill.
>>>Do you want to leave work early Friday and play golf? Let me know!—Jim

Getting Along without Underscoring, Italics, and Boldface

The matter of where lines end is not the only point on which different email programs may have trouble cooperating. Your email program might do boldface and italics, but the program Uncle Fred uses (to once again invoke our favorite relative) might not have a clue how to interpret those typographical expressions. This incompatibility can lead to garbled messages. Your best bet in sending email, as I suggested above, is to keep it unadorned. Well, not exactly stark nekkid, but at least dressed down. The thought and its clear expression are what count, not the finery of "rich text" formatting. Better to be plain and understood than fancy and baffling.

Even with the limitations of plain text, there are certain techniques you can use to provide emphasis or to suggest such conventional typographical effects as italics. Asterisks are handy in this respect. One widely-employed tactic in plain-text email is the use of asterisks for emphasis:

I am going to be *delighted* when I finish this *dreadful* assignment!

An asterisk before and after the word or two you want to stress will be recognized almost universally among emailers as a sign of emphasis.

You can also indicate underscoring of a word or phrase like this:

John and I absolutely _refuse_ to read _Moby Dick_ one more time!

I would be more inclined to put that sentence this way, using asterisks and the journalistic convention of placing book titles in quotation marks. The effect is clear, and the look is better:

John and I absolutely *refuse* to read "Moby Dick" one more time!

All Right, Let's Get On with It!

If you have persevered and read this part of the guide from beginning to end before jumping into the email game itself, I admire your stamina and patience. If you're like me, you read this part some time after you went to the heart of the matter: getting your email in gear. For the patient, be glad: You can now proceed to one email system or another, with a few tools in hand. Let's turn to some popular systems, now, one by one. Again, what we'll be looking at here, for the most part, will be the basics, not the most intimate, intricate details of the systems under consideration. All the systems under consideration feature Help functions, some of them exceptionally detailed, that will provide guidance on the fine points. When in doubt in any system, click Help and see what the system's designers have tucked away to lend you on-the-spot assistance.

Happy emailing!

Emailer's Advisory:

Thanks to the intense competition among the many players offering free email services, this area of the Internet changes rapidly. Old programs evolve and even disappear as new ones become available. Information in this book was current as of February 2002; any of the programs it describes or Web site URLs it lists may change without warning. Nevertheless, chances are good that the basic look and procedures of a free email program will not change radically, in a single evolutionary leap.

If a given URL proves unresponsive, the Web site may still exist, and may be identifiable through a search engine focusing on the name of the site or on a word or phrase pertinent to it.

PART TWO

Some Popular Web-Based Email Systems

MSN HOTMAIL

Microsoft's Hotmail is one of the most popular free Web email programs. It is easy to use, and provides one feature that is far from universal among free Web email programs: automatic checking for viruses of both incoming and outgoing file attachments. If you anticipate sending attachments frequently, that feature alone is a strong argument for using Hotmail rather than a program requiring more complicated and tedious checking for viruses. Hotmail also includes an excellent filter to keep spam out of your inbox—another strong point in its favor.

Creating a New Account

Have your browser go to *http://hotmail.com*. You will see Hotmail's opening page:

Click **Sign Up**

The Hotmail registration screen opens with spaces for your name, language, address, and other routine data. It continues with an **Account Information** section in which you will establish a sign-in name and a password.

41

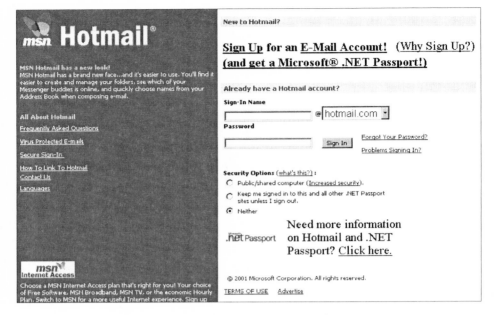

Hotmail's opening page—click *Sign Up* to get started.

As with other email services, you may need to try a number of sign-in names before you find one that has not already been claimed. You may be surprised that what you thought was an original sign-in name is already part of another Hotmail user's account! Be patient, and try to choose a sign-in name that you can live with comfortably and remember easily.

When you first sign in, you will see the system's Terms of Use and Notices. You will need to click **I Accept** at the bottom of the screen to continue. If you do accept, you will have an opportunity to sign up for free newsletters and other online goodies by clicking check-boxes on the next couple of pages.

Login

At Hotmail's opening page, enter your sign-in name and password and click **Sign In**.

Receiving Mail

You are eager to send mail, but first let's see how to get mail. It may be more blessed to give than to receive in most situations, but there's something about opening fresh mail that trumps sending it.

To check your mail, click the **Inbox** tab on the Hotmail opening page, or click the Inbox link under "Message Summary" at the left side of the page. Your inbox will appear on the next page. The Hotmail inbox shows the source of your message in the **From** column, its topic in the **Subject** column, when it was sent in the **Date** column, and how much space it consumes in the **Size** column.

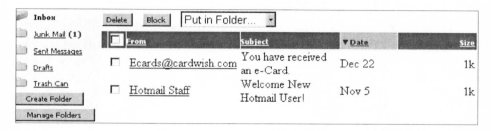

A Hotmail inbox message list.

Click on the underlined link in the **From** column to open a message. Here is an open Hotmail message:

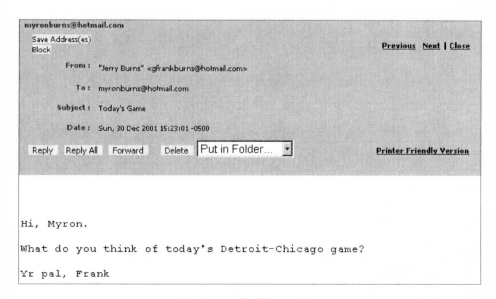

An open received message.

Replying to Mail

One of the handy features of email is that it lets you include your correspondent's message in the reply you send. This ability is especially useful in business correspondence, since it allows everyone who reads the messages to follow the history of the discussion on a particular topic. You've heard of "paper trails." Email makes electronic trails easy to follow, provided correspondents follow what have become standard practices in emailing. The most routine of these practices, in a reply to an email, is to place one's reply at the top of the message heap, so that you end up with related messages in reverse chronological order. Sometimes email messages and replies can include several (even many!) messages; it makes it much easier to follow the discussion if all messages are in reverse chronological order, from the bottom message up.

Let's reply to the message above:

Click on **Reply** (the small box at bottom left, below the Date line).

The Reply message page will appear, with the original message in the message field, marked with the ">" symbol to indicate its sequence in the email exchange. "Re:" ("Regarding") precedes the original subject line. You may leave all of the original message in place, or highlight and delete all or portions of it. It usually is helpful to leave enough of the original message in place to help its sender understand the context of your reply.

Put your cursor on the first line of the original message and press the **Enter** key a few times to give yourself some room to write above the sender's message. Type in your message.

Before you send your message, check the spelling:

Click **Tools** in the pull-down menu at the left, above the message field

Click **Spell Check** in the pull-down menu

As you see below, Hotmail caught the typo in this little football message. To make the correction, I'll click on "quarterback" in the **Suggestions** box, then click the **Change** button. The system will return to the message after spell checking is complete.

When you are happy (or at least satisfied) with your message, click **Send.** Off it will go, including the original message, to your correspondent. The system will confirm your message on a page that tells you it has been sent, and will list the addresses to which it went.

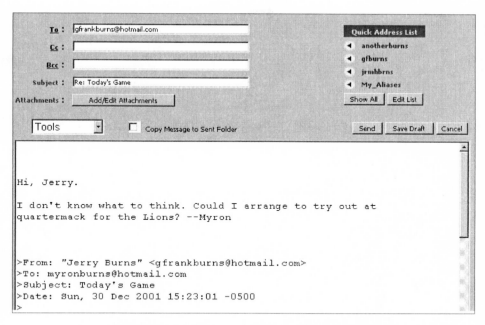

A brief reply to the previous message—with a little problem.

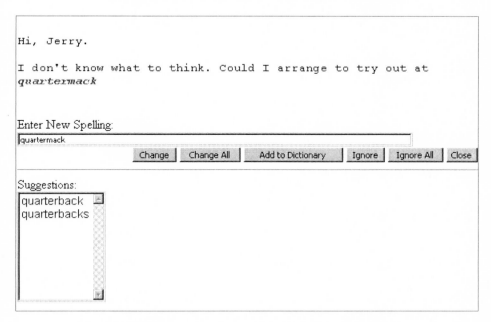

Here Hotmail's spell checker finds a mistake, and suggests a correction.

Composing and Sending a Message

Open the Hotmail Inbox. Click the **Compose** tab. You'll see a composition page headed like the one below:

Heading fields at the beginning of a fresh Hotmail composition page.

Enter the basics: a valid email address in the **To** field, the topic of the message in the **Subject** field, and your message. Check the spelling, as in the reply example above. When you're done, click **Send**. If you change your mind before sending, click **Cancel**, which discards the message and returns you to the Inbox.

Saving Copies of Sent Messages

Hotmail will save copies of your sent messages in your **Sent** folder for up to 30 days. You do not have to create the **Sent** folder manually; the system does it automatically. On the **Compose** page, click the check box next to **Copy Message to Sent Folder**.

To see messages in the **Sent** folder, click the **Sent Messages** folder in the Inbox. (Click **Show Folders** if you do not see your folders listed.)

Sending to Multiple Recipients

To send a message to more than one address at a time, enter the addresses in the To field. Separate the addresses with a semicolon and a space, or a comma and a space. Then proceed as usual.

Saving a Draft

Hotmail makes it easy to save a draft of a message that you would like to finish later. At an open message, like the one below, click the **Save Draft** button (above the message field at the far right).

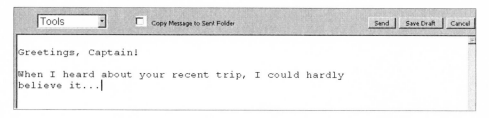

Click *Save Draft* to save the message for further work before sending.

Hotmail will save your message-in-progress in the **Drafts** folder. To retrieve the message so that you can resume work on it, click **Drafts** on the left side of your Inbox. The messages you currently have in draft form will appear in a list in your Drafts folder. Click the address in the **To** column to open your message and continue composition.

Sending Copies

Notice in the Hotmail composition page the **Cc** and **Bcc** boxes. These abbreviations are curious holdovers from the hardcopy age, referring to "carbon copy" and "blind carbon copy." There is no carbon involved here, but if you want to send a copy of your message to someone—and want the primary recipient to know that you sent the copy—enter the email address of the copied recipient in the **Cc** box. If you prefer that the primary recipient not know that you are sending a copy to someone else, enter the copied party's email address in the **Bcc** box.

Forwarding Mail

To forward mail that you have received to another party, open the message that you want to forward.

Click **Forward** just below the message's Date line.

Hotmail will provide the original message in a new composition screen and a fresh set of headers. Enter in the **To** field the addresses of those to whom you want to forward the message. Add your own introduction or commentary in the composition screen above the original message. When ready, click **Send**.

Deleting Mail

At your Hotmail Inbox, if you want to delete a message, click the box before the **From** column for the message you want to delete.

Click the **Delete** button just above and slightly to the left of the **From** column. The message will disappear, but it is not irretrievable. It loiters around for a while in the **Trash Can** folder. Do not linger yourself, however, if you change your mind and want to retrieve it. Hotmail empties the Trash Can several times a week, and then whatever was there is gone. Hotmail, by the way, does not—in contrast to a number of other systems—count space consumed by messages in the Trash Can folder against your account limit. Here is a message in my Inbox that I have checked for deletion:

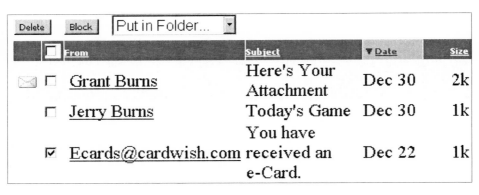

Click on the check box to mark a message for deletion, then click *Delete* at the upper left.

Printing Mail

Hotmail provides a **Printer Friendly** function that makes your messages more convenient to print. To print a message:

Open the message.

Click **Printer Friendly Version** above the message, toward the right side of the page.

Click **File** on your browser's menu bar.

Click **Print**

Complete your print command as you normally would with your browser. (Hotmail Help notes that if your browser is older than Internet Explorer 4.0 or Netscape Navigator 4.08, you can print by copying and pasting a message into a word processor, and print the message from the word processor file.)

Working with Folders

Hotmail comes with several default folders, including the **Inbox, Junk Mail, Sent Messages, Drafts,** and **Trash Can.** You will almost certainly want to create additional folders to help you organize your email. Even if you create only a handful of folders in which to disperse your messages, you will before long find that much more helpful than leaving all your messages in the Inbox and Sent folders. It will be far easier for you to identify messages by topic. If you become a frequent emailer—and many people find this a habit that takes hold quickly—you will probably want to create a fair number of folders to help you maintain electronic order in your life.

Creating a Folder

At your Hotmail Inbox, click the **Create Folder** button at the left of the message list.

At the following page, assign your new folder a name, as I did here:

New Folder Name: |My Business

OK Cancel

Creating a new folder, "My Business."

The Hotmail folders—including the "My Business" folder just created.

Give your new folder name a little thought. As your folders proliferate—and they almost certainly will—careless folder naming will make it harder and harder for you to determine where you put a message, or what you meant by the name of a given folder. Good folder names bear an explicit relation to the messages that they contain. Avoid names like "Folder One," "Folder Two," "Random Stuff," and other such ambiguous terms. Such folder designations may work for a little while, but when you have dozens of folders they will get in your way.

I entered "My Business" as my new folder name, clicked **OK**, and Hotmail returned me to my Inbox. It lists all my folders, including My Business.

Saving Mail to a Folder

Open the message you want to save in a folder. Click the scroll-down **Put in Folder** menu.

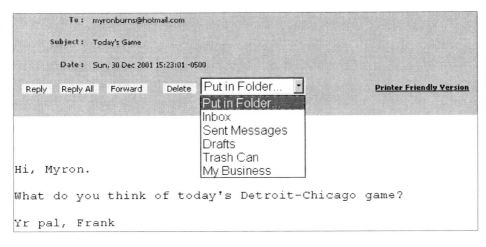

Opening the pull-down *Put in Folder* menu.

Click the folder where you want your message to go. Hotmail will move it there.

To Look at Messages in a Folder

At the Inbox, click the folder name in the left-hand menu. Hotmail will show you a list of the messages in that folder, just as it does in your Inbox. To see a message that you have saved in the folder, click the underlined link in the **From** column, as you do in your Inbox. The message will open.

Saving Mail on Disk

All free email programs have limitations on the amount of online space that you can use. If you save a lot of email, you will want to keep it on disk, either on your hard drive or on floppy disks (or both). When my daughter started college, she promptly became a prolific email sender. I saved almost all of the emails she sent home for four years on a series of floppy disks. Some day, she may find it interesting to track her college experience and her development as an adult by looking through those emails. Or, she may glance at them, roll her eyes, and erase them all. It's her choice—but the choice wouldn't be there if I had not taken a little extra time to store her mail on those disks.

To Save a Message

Use Internet Explorer version 4.0 or later or Netscape Navigator version 4.08 or later.

Open the message.

Click **Printer Friendly Version**

Click **File** on the browser menu bar.

Click **Save As**

Specify the place to save the message. You can save it, for example, as a document in a word processing program, or you can save it on a floppy disk in your A: drive.

Assign a good name to the message.

Click **Save**

You can designate the type of file in which you save your message. If you are saving from the Printer Friendly Version in Hotmail, a plain-text file is a good choice.

Working with Attachments

An attachment is a previously-existing file that you include with an email. The attachment might be a word-processed document, a spreadsheet table, an illustration that you downloaded from the Web, an audio file, or another kind of computer file.

Hotmail automatically checks both outgoing and incoming files for viruses with McAfee VirusScan. The system promises in its Help function that "only files that contain no viruses or a virus that can be cured by McAfee VirusScan are allowed to be attached to files or downloaded from Hotmail." This is a great asset for peace-of-mind emailing.

To Add an Attachment

With your message open, click **Add/Edit Attachments** just below the Subject field.

You will see the following page:

Attach a file to your message in two steps, repeating the steps as needed to attach multiple files. Click **OK** to return to your message when you are done.

1. Click **Browse** to select the file, or type the path to the file
in the box below.

2. Move the file to the **Attachments** box by clicking **Attach**. File Transfer times vary (30 seconds up to 10 minutes).

Find File:

[   ] [Browse..]   [Attach]   Attachments:
                                                                          -- Message Attachments --
                                                          [Remove]

Total size = **OK** (1024K maximum)

Here's where you begin to add an attachment to your message.

I have always found it easier to browse for the file I want to attach than to type the correct path, but you may find the reverse. If you want to browse, click **Browse** at the above screen. Identify the place in your computer where the desired file is. My file, "Resume," is on a floppy disk, so I had my computer look for it in the A: drive.

Click on the file name

Click **Open**

The name of the file will appear in the **Find File** box:

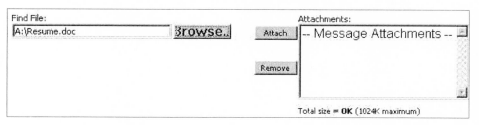

I have selected a file on my floppy disk in the A: drive.

Click **Attach**

Assuming that Hotmail does not detect a virus, when the attachment name appears in the **Attachments** window, click OK below that window. You will then see your message screen with the attachment you opened indicated in the Attachments field, like this:

To :	captstormfield@hotmail.com
Cc :	
Bcc :	
Subject :	Your attachment, Captain!
Attachments :	Resume.doc (21k) Add/Edit Attachments

Hotmail shows that my file, Resume.doc, has been added as an attachment to this message.

Click **Send** to send the message with the attachment.

To View an Attachment

If you have received a message with an attachment and want to see the attachment, click on the name of the attachment.

The system let me know, after scanning it automatically for viruses, that the attached file below was clean. From this point, I would click **Download File** and either open the file or save it to a disk.

Hotmail automatically scans all attachments for viruses using McAfee. Click on the Download File button to download the attachment to your computer, or click Cancel to return to the message.

Name of File	Virus Scan Result
Blakely.doc	✓ No Virus Found

Download File   Cancel

The attachment Blakely.doc checked out virus free.

Working with the Address Book

The Address Book is a helpful feature for quick and easy addressing of messages to individuals or groups. To use it, you will need to add addresses (or "contacts") to it.

To Add an Individual Contact to the Address Book

Click the **Save to My Address Book** check box on a Sent Message confirmation page.

Your message has been **instantly delivered** via
Hotmail*Direct* to the following recipient(s):

                    captstormfield@hotmail.com

Save to my
Address Book
☐

OK

To add Captain Stormfield to my Address Book, I'll click the check box and then click *OK*.

Or, on an open message that you received, click **Save Address(es)** at the top of the message header, and click **OK** at the following page, which confirms the addition to your Address Book

Or, click the **Address Book** tab in any folder; click **Create New**. You will see the following:

Name	*REQUIRED
Quickname* [＿＿＿＿＿＿]	**Quickname** allows you to quickly address messages without typing a full address.
First* [＿＿＿＿＿＿] Last* [＿＿＿＿＿＿]	

E-mail Address	optional

Primary
Address

⦿ **Personal** [＿＿＿＿＿＿＿＿＿＿]

○ **Business** [＿＿＿＿＿＿＿＿＿＿]

○ **Other** [＿＿＿＿＿＿＿＿＿＿]

Note: Mail addressed using a **Quickname** will be sent to the **Primary Address**

Type into the boxes provided information to create a new Address Book entry.

You will see a page on which you can enter information on your new contact. Most of the information is optional, including the email address, but without that address the utility of the Address Book entry is greatly diminished.

When you have finished entering information in the fields on this page, click the OK box at the bottom of the page.

To Add a Group to the Address Book

Click **Address Book**

Click **Groups** tab (at the far right above your listed individual contacts)

Click **Create New**. You will see the following page:

Name	*REQUIRED
Group Name* [＿＿＿＿＿＿＿＿＿＿]	**Group Name** allows you to quickly address messages without typing multiple e-mail addresses.

Members	*REQUIRED

To add members to a group, type their e-mail addresses (separated by a space or comma) in the box below.

Group Members* [＿＿＿＿＿＿＿＿＿＿＿＿＿＿＿]

OK   Cancel

Here's where you establish a group entry in the Address Book.

Enter a name for the group. (Do not use spaces; substitute an under-score or a hyphen for a space, like this: Book_Circle.)

Enter the email addresses of group members; separate addresses with a space or comma. When done, click **OK**.

To Send Mail to Individuals Using the Address Book

Click **Address Book**

Click the checkbox next to the name of the person to whom you want to send your message.

Click **Send Mail**

The system enters the recipient's address in the To field in a fresh composition page. Continue with the message as usual.

To Send Mail to a Group Using the Address Book

Click **Address Book**

Click **Groups**

Click the checkbox next to the group to which you want to send your message.

Click **Send Mail**

The system will complete the To field in a fresh composition page. Write and send your message as usual. Don't forget to enter a descriptive word or term in the Subject field.

The Quick Address List

In the composition page, under the **Quick Address List** box, click the entry for the person or group to which you want to send your message. Hotmail completes the To field with the relevant address(es). This is a very handy function for addressing people to whom you regularly send email. Here is a Quick Address List composed of various close personal friends I established for myself:

Some imaginary Quick Addresses in my Hotmail. You'll want to create *real* Quick Addresses!

Don't Forget the Junkmail Filter!

Unless you're so hungry for email that you want to hear from every pitiful purveyor of spam blighting the Internet, you'll want to set up your junkmail filter soon after establishing your Hotmail account. I forgot to set up my junkmail filter when I started my account; when I returned to it a couple of weeks later, I was astounded at the smut and stupidity that awaited me when I opened my Inbox. This was my fault, not Hotmail's; I left the door open to this stuff. I didn't open any of the "Make Money Fast" or "XXX" appeals, but life is too short to spend any of it deleting this garbage. To keep it out of *your* life when you're using Hotmail:

Click **Options** (to the right of the Address Book tab in any folder).

Click **Junk Mail Filter**

Read the descriptions of the filtering levels, and click on your choice. I suggest **High**.

Click **OK**

Block That Spammer!

I found after putting my junk mail filter in place at the High setting that I received almost nothing in the way of spam. Although this filter is very effective, there is another option that you might want to put into effect, the **Block** function. This feature allows you to block email from specific senders or domains. To activate it, at the Inbox, click the checkboxes next to the addresses you do not want to hear from again. To block email from a whole domain (the source indicated by the term following the "@" symbol in an email address), click only one checkbox by a message from that domain. Click **Block** above the message list, and follow ensuing instructions. If you have been receiving email from a pest who is not stymied by the Junk Mail Filter, the Block should keep him, her, or it out of your Inbox.

POP Mail Retrieval Settings

Do you have an email account using the POP (Post Office Protocol) through your employer, organization, or an Internet Service Provider? Hotmail allows you to retrieve mail automatically from up to four of those accounts.

Other Useful Options

Hotmail offers many other useful functions that you can access from the Options page, including language (send your messages in Chinese or Swedish, assuming you know how to write in those languages); "Safe List" creation, which prevents messages from specified addresses from ever being treated as junkmail; custom filters, to route incoming messages to specified folders; and many others.

Help

Hotmail's Help function allows access through an All Topics list, as well as through a search ("Find") feature that enables you to enter specific words and phrases to locate throughout the Help system.

Remember to Sign Out!

When you're through using Hotmail, click the Sign Out button in the upper right corner of the screen. This is something to pay particular attention to if you are using Hotmail at a publicly accessible computer. Safe computing practices do not include walking away from your email system and leaving it open to someone else to use!

MAIL.COM

Mail.com, a free service of net2phone, claims to have the largest standard mailbox of any free Web-based email program. At its lusty 10MB, it would be hard to line up challengers to this claim. Mail.com is very straightforward and simple to use. To get there from here, have your Internet browser go to Mail.com's sign-in page, *http://www.mail.com*. Click **GO** next to **New Member Sign-Up** on the left side of the screen. You'll go to this page:

Mail.com offers a wide range of domains for a more personalized email address.

Creating an Account

Type a user name in the box on the left side of the page. Click on a domain name in the right-hand menu to complete your email address. You can be as unadorned as mail.com, or as personal as loveable.com.

Click **Next Page**. You will see a page that starts like this:

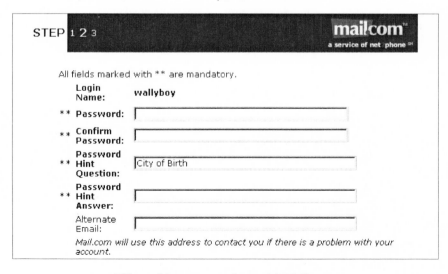

Fill out this page to register with Mail.com.

You will need to click on a check box at the bottom of the page indicating that you have read and will comply with Mail.com's terms and conditions.

Mail.com terms and conditions >click here
I have read the terms and conditions and agree by them. ☑

Sign Me Up   Reset

If you click on *click here*, you'll see Mail.com's terms and conditions.

Click **Sign Me Up**. The next page gives you a chance to sign up for various services, some free, some not. You do not have to sign up for any of them. When you see the following statement at the bottom of this page, click on the statement.

Your account is now active!
Click here to log in.

It may take a minute or two for this statement to appear; be patient.

The Mail.com navigation bar

Logging In

At the Mail.com sign-in page, log in with the complete email address you established in your sign-up procedure. Type your Mail.com password in the second box, and click **Log-In**.

The following page is your chief base of operations in Mail.com. On the left side of the screen, in particular, are the navigation bar links that enable you to negotiate the system's features.

Retrieving Messages

Click **Get New Messages** on the main navigation bar. That will take you to the Mail.com inbox, which looks like this:

INBOX - 2 Message(s), 2 Unread   **External Mail Empty Trash**

	From	Subject	Date >>	Size
☐	"Grant Burns"	**Bad Storm Coming!**	25 Feb 2002	1k
☐	Mail.com Member Services	**Welcome to Mail.com**	25 Feb 2002	1k

[Move To] [Drafts ▾] [Delete]   [Showing 1 to 2 of 2]

[Select All] [Deselect All]

[Move To] [Drafts ▾] [Delete]   [Showing 1 to 2 of 2]

I'm so popular; I get messages from myself and from my email provider.

New (or, at any rate, unopened) messages have their From fields bold-faced, to make them easy to spot. Click on the subject line to open a message. Here is an open message; the headers indicate the sender, subject, and date of sending:

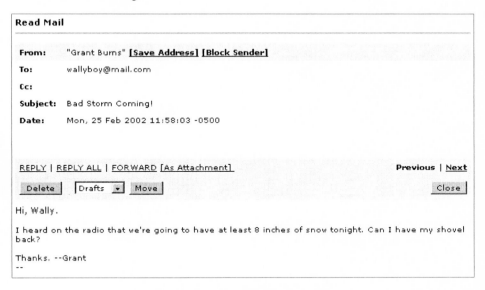

Read Mail

From: "Grant Burns" **[Save Address] [Block Sender]**
To: wallyboy@mail.com
Cc:
Subject: Bad Storm Coming!
Date: Mon, 25 Feb 2002 11:58:03 -0500

REPLY | REPLY ALL | FORWARD [As Attachment]   **Previous | Next**

[Delete] [Drafts ▾] [Move]   [Close]

Hi, Wally.

I heard on the radio that we're going to have at least 8 inches of snow tonight. Can I have my shovel back?

Thanks. --Grant
--

An open Mail.com message

To close the message, click **Close** in the lower-right corner. Doing so will return you to the inbox.

Replying to a Message

With a message open, click on **Reply** in the area below the headers. Click Reply All if the original message went to multiple recipients, and you want them all to receive your reply.

Mail.com sets up the reply screen like this:

```
┌──────────────────────────────────────────────────────────────────────┐
│  Send    │ │  Save Draft  │                  Importance : │ normal  ▼ │
│                                                                        │
│ Please click to select names from your Address Book                   │
│                                                                        │
│ To:       │"Grant Burns" <gfburns@mail.com>                         │ │
│                                                                        │
│ Cc:       │                            │   Bcc:  │                   │ │
│                                                                        │
│ Subject:  │Re: Bad Storm Coming!                                    │ │
│                                                                        │
│ ┌──────────────────────────────────────────────────────────────┬─▲─┐ │
│ │-----Original Message-----                                      │   │ │
│ │From: "Grant Burns" <gfburns@mail.com>                          │   │ │
│ │Date: Mon, 25 Feb 2002 11:58:03 -0500                           │   │ │
│ │To: wallyboy@mail.com                                           │   │ │
│ │Subject: Bad Storm Coming!                                      │   │ │
│ │                                                                │   │ │
│ │> Hi, Wally.                                                    │   │ │
│ │>                                                               │   │ │
│ │> I heard on the radio that we're going to have at least 8 inches of snow │
│ │tonight. Can I have my shovel back?                             │   │ │
│ │>                                                               │   │ │
│ │> Thanks. --Grant                                               │   │ │
│ │> --                                                            │ ▼ │ │
│ └──────────────────────────────────────────────────────────────┴───┘ │
└──────────────────────────────────────────────────────────────────────┘
```

When replying to a message, start your reply *above* the original.

The sender's address appears automatically in the To field, and the original subject line appears in the Subject field, preceded by Re: ("Regarding").

Click in the message field just above the headers for the original message field. Press the Enter key two or three times to create a little space between the original message and your response.

Type your reply. If you're uncertain about your spelling, double-check questionable words. (Keep a good dictionary in reach, if possible.) No one likes to receive emails with sloppy spelling.

When you are satisfied that your message is clearly stated, and free of spelling errors, click **Send** in the upper-left corner of the screen. Mail.com will take you back to your inbox, and above it will post a brief note letting you know that "Your Mail Has Been Sent."

Composing and Sending a Message

Sending a fresh message is much like sending a reply. In the main navigation bar, click **Write Message**. The system will open a fresh Write Message screen:

```
Write Message

 Send    Save Draft                              Importance : [normal ▼]
 Please click to select names from your Address Book

 To:    [                                                              ]

 Cc:    [                        ]    Bcc: [                    ]

 Subject: [                                                            ]

        [                                                         ▲]
        [                                                          ]
        [                                                          ]
        [                                                          ]
        [                                                         ▼]
```

The excitement of a fresh message screen—ready for a note to a friend, or to the White House.

Type a valid email address in the To field. Press the Tab key to move the cursor down to the Subject field, and type in a word or phrase that reasonably describes the contents of the message. Good subject headings are especially important for both you and your recipient if either of you saves email for an extended time. After a few days, or a few weeks, the content of messages in a list that sports the subject headers "Hi!" or "What's Up?" are not easy to guess.

Type your message. Reread it for clarity; be alert for typos and spelling errors. When everything looks ship-shape, click Send.

Sending Messages to Multiple Recipients

Enter multiple addresses in the To field; separate the addresses with commas.

Saving a Draft of a Message

Mail.com makes it easy to save a draft of a message for later work. This can be handy when you're writing a difficult message, when you find that you need to check a detail (what *were* those third quarter sales figures, anyhow?), or must interrupt yourself for another reason. Lunch, for example.

At any point during composition, click **Save Draft** at the top of the Write Message screen. The system automatically saves the message-in-progress in your Draft folder, and returns you to your inbox.

To retrieve a draft, click **Draft** in the navigation bar, click on the subject of the draft message to open it, and go back to composing the message as usual.

Sending Copies

Sometimes you will want to send a message to someone(s) other than the primary recipient(s). Primary recipients' email addresses should appear only in the To field. Address secondary recipients—those with a less than immediate interest in or need to know about the message—in the Cc or Bcc field. You are not really sending "carbon copies" or "blind carbon copies," as you might have back in the typewriter day, but the effect is the same.

Exercise some caution with the Bcc field. No one else addressed in the message will be aware of anyone addressed in this field. It isn't good to develop a reputation as someone who routinely sends copies of messages on the sly, but sometimes discretion does call for use of the Bcc field.

Forwarding Messages

It is easy to forward a message that you have received to another party. With the message open, click **Forward** (just to the right of Reply and Reply All). A Write Message screen will appear, with the original message in the message field (preceded by the original headers, including the sender and date), and the original subject heading in the new Subject field, preceded by **Fw** ("Forward").

Type into the To field the email address of anyone to whom you wish to forward the original message. Before you click Send, it would be helpful if you would include in the message field, above the original message, a little introduction to help orient your recipients to the forwarding.

Keep in mind that although forwarding messages is often good form, not every message was meant to be forwarded, especially not without the sender's permission. Please see my comments on this subject in this guide's first part.

Deleting Messages

If the message is open, click **Delete**, above the message field. Mail.com moves the message into the Trash Folder.

To delete a message from the message list in a folder, click the **check box** to the left of the message line and click **Delete**. The message goes into the Trash. I've clicked on the check box next to the first message below; clicking on Delete will place the message in the Trash.

Click the check box, then click Delete to get rid of a message.

The system regularly empties messages in the Trash folder, so don't put anything there that might be a keeper. Mail.com suggests creating a separate folder to store messages that might be Trashable—but may not. You could call it your Almost Trash folder, or your Not Quite Trash folder.

Printing Messages

To print a message, open it as usual. User your browser's print function as you would in other circumstances.

Working with Folders

Folders are places to put messages. A good folder system greatly enhances the effectiveness of your email management. Mail.com's default folders include the Inbox, Sent Mail, Draft, and Trash. You may create as many additional, personal folders as you wish to help you manage your email. If you send and receive any appreciable amount of email, you will find that the default folders simply will not do for the long run of good message organization.

To Create a Folder

Click on **Personal Folders** in the navigation bar. You will see a page with these details:

Folders

Folder Name	No. of Messages	Unread	Size
Drafts	0	0	0k
INBOX	2	1	3k
SENT	0	0	0k
Trash	0	0	0k

Create Folders

[   ] [Create]

Delete Folders

[▾] [Delete]

Rename Folders

Rename [▾] To [   ] [Done]

The Folders list provides details on the contents of individual folders.

Type a name for your new folder in the **Create Folders** box. Make the name a tight fit with the contents you anticipate putting into the folder. "Miscellaneous" is not good!

Click **Create**. The new folder will be included in your overall folder roster.

To access any folders that you have created, click Personal Folder in the main navigation bar. All your folders will appear in the folder list, like the one above.

Click on any folder's name to enter it and work with the messages it contains.

Saving Messages to a Folder

In a folder's message list, click the check box to the left of the message(s) in question.

Click on the arrow to open the folder menu above or below the message list:

With the message checked and a folder selected in the pull-down menu, I can move the message to another place.

Click on a folder name to select it.

Click **Move To**

Mail.com will move the check-marked message to the designated folder.

Saving Messages to Disk

You may save a message to your hard drive or to a floppy disk for long-term storage, or to scan for viruses if it contains an attachment. With the message open, use your browser's File/Save As feature. Here I am saving a message in my **A:** drive. I clicked **File** in the upper-left corner of the screen, then **Save As** to open the **Save As** dialog box. I opened the **Save in** menu and clicked on **A:**. Clicking **Save** will save the message on my floppy disk, from which I can open it in the future.

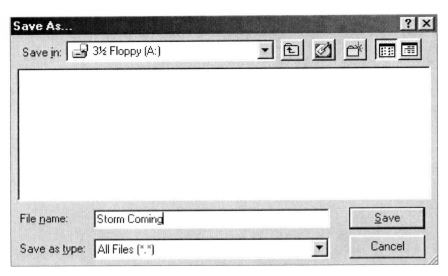

About to save a message on a floppy disk

Working with Attachments

An attachment is a file that accompanies an email message and that the recipient opens using the relevant software on his or her computer. A file may be a text document, a song or movie clip, a picture, or another type of computer product.

To Create an Attachment

Click **Browse** below the open message to open the **File Upload** window

Find the desired file and click on it to highlight it

Click **Open**. The file will appear in the Step 1 box.

Click **Attach**. The file name will appear in the Attachment window. (At the same time, the file name will disappear from the box in Step 1.)

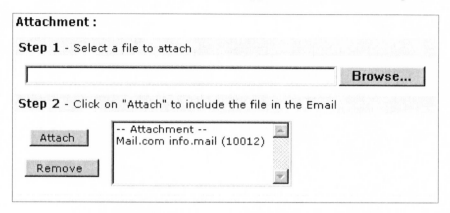

The attachment name appears in the second box.

To View an Attachment

Do not open any attachment unless you are confident that it does not contain a virus.

File attachments are the leading mode of transmission for computer viruses, and no message source, not even your own mother, can be fully trusted to send you virus-free attachments. It is very easy to send viruses without intending to do so. To practice safe emailing, save your message with the attachment to disk and scan it with a virus detector and repair program before opening it. (Follow the Saving Messages to Disk directions above.)

If you have saved and scanned the message for viruses and it checks out clean:

Click on the name of the attachment in the message.

When prompted to view the file or save it, select view. If your computer has software able to open the attachment, it

Click on the boldfaced attachment link to proceed.

should go ahead and do that. Remember, though, that it is not the email program, but software on your computer, that opens attachments. If you do not have the necessary software, you will not be able to open the attachment.

Courtesy note: You will stand in good esteem among your email correspondents if you scan your outgoing attachments for viruses before you send them.

Working with the Address Book

The Address Book simplifies the task of sending messages to people whom you frequently address, or to groups. To use the Address Book, you must establish some contacts in it.

To Add a Contact to the Address Book

Click **Address Book** on the navigation bar.

In the Address Book page, click on **Create Personal Contacts.**

Address Book

Call Contact | Create Personal Contacts

Personal Contacts

You'll see this after clicking on Address Book in the navigation bar. (You may also see some advertising at this point.) Click on Create Personal Contacts at the right to proceed.

Type the necessary information in the required fields. You may add information such as street address, phone number, and so on in optional fields.

When done, click **Add Contact.** The system will add the entry to your Address Book.

Personal Address

Alias Name:			
E-mail Address:			
First Name:		Last Name:	
Address:			
City:		State/Province:	
Postal Code:		Country:	
Company Name:			
Home phone:		Work Phone:	
Pager:		Mobile:	
Fax:		Other:	

Birthday: `Jan ▼` `1 ▼` `1900 ▼` (mm/dd/yyyy)

When you add information on a contact, remember to include the email address!

Creating a Mailing List

A mailing list is an easy timesaver for sending frequent messages to the same group of people.

Click **Address Book** on the navigation bar.

Click on **Create Group Contacts** (below Create Personal Contacts).

Assign the group a name.

Type in the email addresses for the group members; separate addresses with commas.

Click **Add Contact.** Your mailing list will be established, like this:

Group Contacts							
To	Cc	Bcc	Name	E-mail Address			
◌	◌	◌	**My Pitching Staff**	hwilhelm@knuckles.com rjohnson@whiff.com skoufax@lefty.com wjohnson@heavenly.net	**Call Contact**	**Modify Contact**	**Delete Contact**

Most managers could live with a pitching staff like this one.

The Address Book Alias

The Alias function is another easy timesaver. When you add a contact, you can assign an "alias," or nickname. If you assign your friend James Johnson the alias "Jim" in the Address Book, in the future you can address messages to him simply by typing "Jim" (without the quote marks) in the To field.

Addressing Messages with the Address Book

With a Write Message page open, click **Address Book** above the To field to open the Address Book.

Click to check the box (To, Cc, or Bcc) by the email address(es) of anyone to whom you would like to send the message.

Click **OK** to go back to the Write Message page and include the selected addressee(s) in the desired field.

Click on the check boxes to address a message.

Fine Tuning Your Mail.com

Mail.com offers a healthy range of fine-tuning features, from automatic replies (great when you're on vacation and not tending your email) to filters that let you block particular senders from entering your inbox, as well as enabling you to route incoming messages to specific folders. Click on **Options** in the navigation bar to see capsule descriptions of the possibilities:

Options

Change Password

Change your password in order to maintain security for your Mail.com account.

External Mail

Collect E-mail from all of your external E-mail accounts into one convenient location.

Mail Filters

Mail filters allow you to block incoming mail from addresses you have specified; in addition, defined types of mail can be automatically sorted into specified folders.

Signature Settings

Defines your signature, or the text that is automatically appended to every E-mail message that you send out with a signature.

Autoreply

The Auto Reply option is used to define, enable, or disable the automatic response mechanism that is triggered by any incoming mail.

Preferences

Customize your personal preferences

Update Email Address

Someone could be looking for you at your old e-mail address. Register with Veripost today and stay connected with friends family and online relationships - for free. You get to control who gets your new e-mail address.

Capsule descriptions of Mail.com options.

The **Preferences** option offers choices on how Mail.com displays your mail, when it empties your Trash folder, whether it automatically saves copies of outgoing messages, and so on. The **External Mail** option allows you to retrieve messages from up to five POP3 mail systems.

Mail.com also offers a number of premium services for various fees, such as a larger mailbox, automatic forwarding, etc.

Logout

When you're through using Mail.com, click **Logout** on the navigation bar. This will prevent others from deliberately or inadvertently using your mail account. Logging out from your Web mail is especially crucial if you're accessing it from a public machine in a library or elsewhere.

NETSCAPE MAIL

Netscape, best known for its popular Web browser, also offers free Web email.

To Create a New Account

At the Netscape home page (*http://netscape.com*), click on **Mail** near the top left of the screen.

At the sign-up page, below, click on **Sign-up**.

Fill out the Netscape Mail registration form. You'll select a screen name and password, provide your name and address, and decide whether you would like Netscape to send you additional product information or share some of your registration data with other companies whose products you might find interesting.

Click **Next** when the system accepts your screen name. Do be patient when selecting a screen name. Millions of people use Netscape Mail; you may find it challenging to devise a screen name that someone else has not already chosen!

The Netscape Mail Sign in/Sign up page. Used with permission.

Login

At the Netscape home page, click on **Mail**.

Enter your screen name and password.

Click **Sign In**

Receiving Mail

At the opening screen of Netscape Mail, click on either **Inbox/Get Mail** or, if you have a new message, on the **New Message** link.

After signing in, the Netscape Mail user receives a prompt alert to any new messages. Used with permission.

Your inbox messages will appear in reverse chronological order. Messages that you have previously read will have a check mark in the box to the left of their subject headers. The inbox will also specify who sent the mail, the date of sending, and the size of the message. Brand new mail will have the symbol of an envelope to the left of the subject header, and the subject header itself will be in boldface. Click the subject line to retrieve a message.

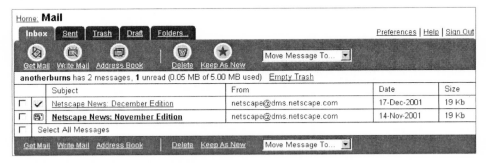

In this Inbox message list, the check mark next to the first message indicates that I have opened it. The subject header of the second message is in boldface, showing that the message has not been opened. Used with permission.

Replying to Mail

With your message open, click **Reply** above and to the right of the message's subject line. (Click **Reply to All** if the original message went to multiple recipients, and you would like all of them to see what you have to say.)

To reply to this message, I will click on *Reply*. Used with permission.

The original message will remain in place, with its sender's name in the **To** field and "**RE:**" ("Regarding") preceding the original subject line. With your cursor at the beginning of the line noting who sent the message, press your **Enter** key a few times to move the original message down in the screen.

To:	jrmhbrns@netscape.net
Cc:	
Bcc:	
Subject:	RE: Greetings to My Alter Ego

Type your message here:

```
jrmhbrns@netscape.net wrote:

>Hello again...
>
>I hope that you're enjoying your new Netscape Mail account!
>
>--Jerry
```

In a reply, the greater-than (>) symbol precedes lines from the original message. Used with permission.

Move your cursor up into the now-free space above the original message, and write your reply. Keep a dictionary handy unless you're an uncommonly gifted speller. If you have doubts about a word, check the dictionary. Emails with bad spelling are commonplace, but do not speak well of a sender's esteem for those who receive them.

When you have finished your reply, including doing your spelling review, click **Send** in the upper left corner of the screen, and the message will go out. Netscape Mail lets you know that your message went out with the following statement:

A reassuring statement after you've clicked *Send*. Used with permission.

Click **OK** to return to your Inbox, or to whichever folder you were in when you sent and composed the message.

Composing and Sending a Message

To start a fresh message, in any folder click **Write Mail** (2d button from the left above the list of messages). In the following page, enter a valid email address in the **To** field and a descriptive subject heading in the **Subject** field. Compose your message in the main body of the page. When you are satisfied with it, click **Send.**

If you change your mind about sending your message, click **Cancel.** Remember: Once you have sent an email, you'll no more be able to get it back than you would a letter that you dropped into a U.S. Mail box. Sent is truly sent (provided you used a functioning email address), so think for a moment before you click on **Send.**

Sending to Multiple Recipients

Separate addresses in the **To** field (or Cc or Bcc fields) with commas.

Saving a Draft

Suppose you have started a message, but cannot complete it just now. That is no problem in Netscape Mail. Click **Save as Draft** (2d button from the right above the message field).

Netscape Mail will save the message you have begun in your **Drafts** folder. (More on folders momentarily.) You can retrieve the message from your Drafts folder, complete it and mail it at your convenience.

Sending Copies

To send a copy of a message to someone other than its primary recipient (the addressee represented on the **To** field), enter the email address to which you want to send a copy in the Cc ("carbon copy") or Bcc ("blind carbon copy") field. Keep in mind that no one listed on the To field will realize that you are sending copies to anyone listed in the Bcc field. This fact entails some potential difficulties—not technological, but social. Please see my comments on copies in this guide's first part.

Forwarding Mail

Like sending copies, forwarding your email correspondents' messages to others can be problematic. For some discussion of the issue, see the section dealing with forwarding in this guide's first part. Forwarding definitely has its proper place, though. To forward a message:

Open the message.

Click **Forward** on the tab toolbar.

You'll see a new Write a Message page open, with the original subject in the subject field. The message you are forwarding will reach your recipient as an attachment, rather than being included in the composition field in the new message.

Enter the address to which you want to forward the message in the To field.

Write a message to accompany and explain, if necessary, the attached forwarding.

Click **Send**

Deleting Mail

It is important to delete old email, not only because old mail clutters your life, but also because Netscape, like other email services, places a limit on your online space. At this writing, Netscape allows you 5MB.

At your **Inbox,** or in another folder, you'll see check boxes at the far left of the list of messages. If you click the check box, and then click **Delete,** the system will send the message to your Trash folder, where you can still retrieve it. You can mark multiple messages in the same folder for deleting, and send them all to the Trash folder with one click on **Delete.** Here I have marked the first message, and will send it packing by clicking **Delete:**

		Subject	From	Date	Size
☑	✓	Greetings to My Alter Ego	Jrmhbrns	2-Jan-2002	1 Kb
☐	✓	Netscape News: December Edition	netscape@dms.netscape.com	17-Dec-2001	19 Kb
☐		**Netscape News: November Edition**	netscape@dms.netscape.com	14-Nov-2001	19 Kb
☐		Select All Messages			

Inbox | Sent | Trash | Draft | Folders...   Preferences | Help | Sign Out

Get Mail   Write Mail   Address Book   Delete   Keep As New   Move Message To... ▾

anotherburns has 3 messages, **1** unread (0.05 MB of 5.00 MB used)   Empty Trash

I no longer need the first message on this list. After clicking the check box at the left, I'll click *Delete* above the message list to make it go away. Used with permission.

If I wanted to delete everything in my Inbox, I would click the box to the left of **Select All Messages**, and then click Delete.

Don't Forget to Take Out the Trash!

Netscape Mail does not automatically empty your Trash folder. You will need to empty it from time to time yourself to avoid wasting your system space on messages that have served their purposes. You may delete items from your Trash folder one by one:

Click on your **Trash** folder to open it.

Click the checkboxes next to any messages you want to delete completely.

Click **Delete**

That's the slow way. To remove *all* messages from your Trash folder:

Click **Preferences** (toward the right corner of the screen, above your message list).

Click **Empty Your Trash Folder** (toward the bottom of the Preferences screen).

Printing Mail

To print a message in Netscape Mail, with the message in question open, print it as you would any file using your browser print function.

Working with Folders

Netscape Mail's default folders are **Inbox, Sent, Trash,** and **Draft**. Unless you seldom use email, you will probably want to make other folders in which to store messages. A good set of folders will do a lot to enhance your emailing experience; it will save you time and confusion. Speaking as someone who once allowed hundreds of messages to languish in my basic in-box, even after reading them, I can speak with the voice of chastened experience when I encourage you not to do the same. You may assign your folders to specific people (your children, e.g.—Jane, John, Alice), to organizations (My Quilting Circle, Rotary, Book Club), or to types of activities or interests represented by messages in the folders (Financial, Hobbies, School).

Creating a Folder

You may create folders from different locations in Netscape Mail. From the Inbox, for example, click the **Folders** tab (just above the Delete button).

On the next screen, click **New Folder**, just below the Folders tab, like this:

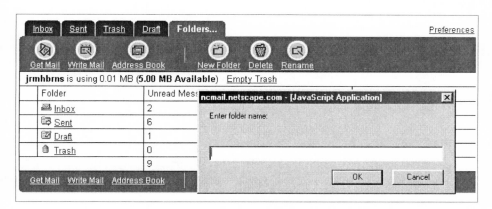

Making a new folder in Netscape Mail. Used with permission.

You will see a box requesting a folder name. Enter a good name. What is a "good" folder name? It needs to be one with a straightforward connection to the messages that will go into the folder. It should be one that will make immediate sense to you even if you do not use it for weeks or possibly months at a time. As your folders multiply—and they often breed at an alarming rate when you get into busy emailing—you will find it frustrating and a waste of time having to figure out what you meant by the folder name "Other Stuff" when you haven't dipped into that folder in several months.

Click **OK**

Your new folder will now appear in your folder list when you click **Folders.**

I created a new folder that I called "Notes on Emailing." Here's what I saw in my folder list after clicking **OK:**

	Folder
	✉ Inbox
	📭 Sent
	📝 Draft
	🗑 Trash
⌒	📁 Notes on E-Mailing

My new folder ("Notes on Emailing") appears in my folder list. Used with permission.

Saving Mail to a Folder

At an open message, pull down the **Move Message To** menu and click on the folder where you want to save this message. Click the folder name. Netscape Mail will move the message into the folder you specified and out of your inbox.

Or, click the checkbox to the left of a message in the message list.

Click on a folder choice from the pull-down **Move Message To** menu.

The selected message will go into the specified folder. If I clicked on "Notes on Emailing" in the screen below, the "Greetings to My Alter Ego" message would go into that folder.

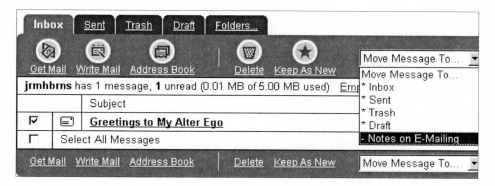

I want to move the first message on this list to the "Notes on Emailing" folder. I clicked the check box to the left of the message, and will click on Notes on Emailing in the drop-down menu. Used with permission.

To Retrieve a Message Saved to a Folder

Click **Folders**

Click the name of the folder where you saved your message.

Click on the subject line of the message in the message list.

Saving Mail to a Disk

Follow the usual procedure for saving a file with your browser. Normally, you will click on **File** in the upper left corner, click **Save As**, and then choose where to save the file in your computer or on a floppy disk.

Working with Attachments

Virus Note: Do not send or open attachments unless you are confident that they are virus free. If you are using an email program that does not check for viruses, please be sure that your computer is equipped with an antivirus program. These programs are available at office supply stores and computer stores. They are not generally very expensive, often under $50, and are easy to install on your computer. The money you spend on one is more than worthwhile: It will help prevent your attachments from infecting other people's computers, not to mention protect your own computer and data from possibly serious damage.

An attachment is a computer file that you include in an email. It could be from a spreadsheet, or a document from your word processor, an illustration you downloaded from the Internet, or almost anything else that fits within the email program's size restrictions (5MB for Netscape Mail).

To Create an Attachment

Click on **Write Mail**

Address, identify with a subject header, and compose your message.

Click **Add** (near **Attachments** window below body of the message).

The **Attach a File** page opens. Enter in the text box the name of the file that you want Netscape Mail to attach to your message. (Or, click **Browse** to search your computer for the file you want to attach.) When I clicked the Browse button here, the File Upload box opened. I wanted to attach a document from a floppy disk in my A: drive, so I selected the Floppy A as the "Look in" site.

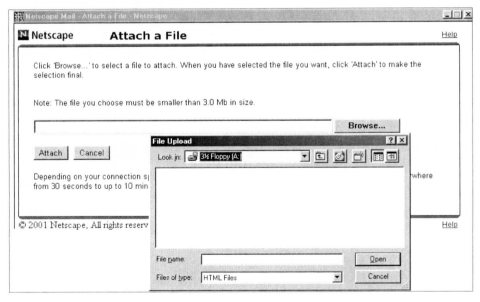

Using the browse function to look for a file to attach. Used with permission.

I have no HTML files on that floppy disk, so no files are listed—but if I scroll down in the **Files of type** menu and select "All Files," see what happens:

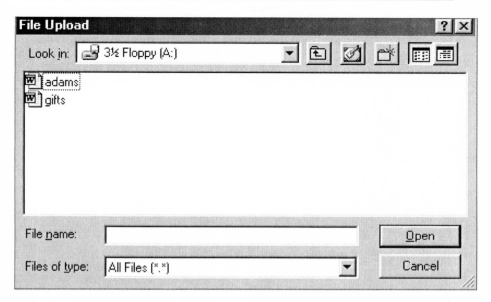

When I select *All Files* in Files of type, I see a list of everything on my floppy disk. Used with permission.

With the name of the attachment accurately typed in the text box in the **Attach a File** box, or the file selected through the Browse function, click **Attach.**

You will see the **Write a Message** page, with the attached file's name in the Attachments window, like this:

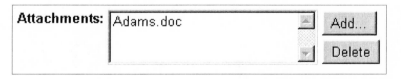

The selected file appears in the Attachments window. Used with permission.

When you are satisfied with your message and your attachment, click **Send.**

To Open an Attachment

(Do not open any attachment before scanning it for viruses.)

Open the message containing the attachment.

Click the name of the attached file next to **Attachment:**

Click **Save File**

In the **Save As** box, select a folder in which to save the file.

Click **Save**

Scan the file (or folder) for viruses with your antivirus software. If the file is clean, open it with the appropriate program (for example, a word processor if the file is a text file).

Working with the Address Book

The address book is a helpful tool that speeds addressing of messages. To use it, you will need to establish some email addresses in your Address Book.

To Add an Address

Click **Address Book** on any tab toolbar. You will see the following box:

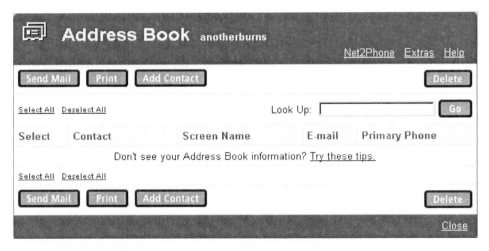

Here's where you start to add an entry in your Address Book. Used with permission.

Click **Add Contact**. You'll see the **New Contact** dialog box appear, like this:

Clicking on the various tabs gives access to space for considerable contact information in the Address Book. Used with permission.

Enter names, email addresses, and, if you wish, telephone numbers for those you want to contact through the Address Book. You may also click on the other tabs and enter further information.

Click **Save**. The entry will appear in your address book.

You can also add an address this way:

Open a message.

Click an address next to **From** or **Cc**. You'll see a **Features Page** open.

Click **Add to Address Book**

The **Add Contact** dialog box opens. Netscape Mail shows the email address and possibly the name, of your contact. Add further information if you wish.

Click **Save**

To Address a Message with the Address Book

Click **Write Mail**

Click **Add Addresses** (just to the right of the Send button; the Recipient List page opens).

Click **To** (or **Cc** or **Bcc**) in front of the Address Book entries to which you want to address the message; here I have checked the box to address a message to my alter ego, Jerry Burns:

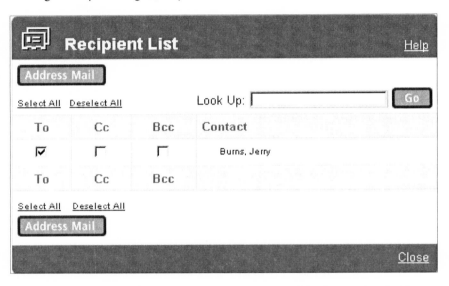

I have clicked the check box to address a message to my friend Jerry. Used with permission.

Click **Address Mail**

The system will take you back to the Write Mail screen, with the To field completed. Complete and send your message as usual. Remember to enter a subject!

Preferences

The Netscape Mail **Preferences** options allow you to include your full name in outgoing messages, and to personalize your outgoing mail with your signature. It also reminds you of how much space you are using in your 5MB system allowance.

Privacy Considerations

Netscape is a certified member of the TRUSTe program, an independent, nonprofit initiative that promotes fair information practices.

Mail Guided Tour

Netscape Mail offers a brief but helpful online Mail Guided Tour of its system. The tour focuses on the basics of getting started, using your inbox, reading mail, creating folders, and so on. It's worth a spin. To try it out, click **Take our Guided Tour** at the bottom of the Netscape Mail Welcome Page.

A Little Help?

Netscape Mail's help function will answer most questions that you have about the system. Click on **Help** from any point in the system.

Sign Out!

Remember to click **Sign Out** (over on the right side of the screen) when you have finished your Netscape Mail session. Signing out is especially important if you are working at a public computer. Signing out will prevent the next user from accidentally or deliberately getting into your email.

YAHOO! MAIL

Yahoo! Mail is, by Web email standards, a full-featured, flexible program. Its basic space allotment to users is generous, too: a full 6MB, which is twice as much as the free space permitted by some other programs. Among its features that are not found in every free email program is internal scanning of both incoming and outgoing attachments for viruses. This is a welcome, timesaving service, and by itself makes Yahoo! Mail worth serious consideration as your preferred Web email system.

Creating a New Account

Have your browser go to *http://www.yahoo.com*. You'll see the Yahoo! portal page.

Click the **Check Email** symbol at the top of the page, third item from the left. That click will take you to this page (Reproduced with permission of Yahoo! Inc. ©2000 by Yahoo! Inc. Yahoo! and the Yahoo! logo are trademarks of Yahoo! Inc.):

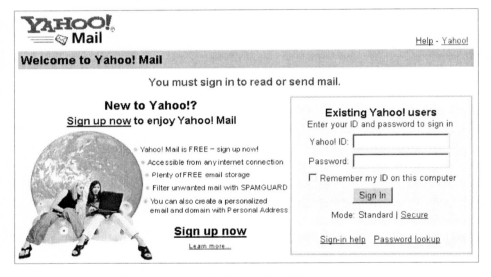

Sign up—or sign in, if you already have an account.

Click on **Sign up now** on the left side of the screen. That click will take you to the **Welcome to Yahoo! Mail** page, where you can choose which Yahoo! Mail service you prefer. Yahoo! lets you indulge your vanity a little bit: For $35 a year, you can have a personalized email address. If you decide to forego the personalized address or the Business Edition (with enhanced features for $9.95/month) for the time being, click on the free edition's **Sign Me Up!** link. That link will take you to a registration form.

When you have completed the form, click **Submit This Form** at the bottom of the form, and you will soon be a Yahoo! Mail user.

Login

To use Yahoo! Mail immediately, return to the sign-in page (*http://mail.yahoo.com*). Enter your Yahoo! ID and password. Click **Sign In**.

After you sign in, Yahoo! takes you to the **Mail Home** page, where you'll see whether you have new messages. You'll also see some advertising, system announcements (Yahoo! was running a virus alert when I wrote this), and other Yahoo! features. To go into the email system itself, click on any of the choices in this menu at the left side of the Mail Home page:

Retrieving a Message

Click **Check Mail** (top left) to see what's waiting for you in your in-box.

The menu...

When I clicked **Check Mail**, Yahoo! Mail showed me this short list of messages:

Check Other Mail	Empty Trash			showing 1-2 of 2

Delete	checked mail		- Choose Folder - ▾	Move

	Sender	▾ **Date**	**Size**	**Subject**
☐	G.F. Burns	Mon 10/29	14k 📎	Here's that attachment!
☐	Yahoo!	Thu 09/06	445b	Welcome to Yahoo! Mail

A message list in the Yahoo! Mail in-box. The bold-faced message has not been opened.

The main columns in Yahoo! Mail indicate the sender of the message, the date it was sent, the amount of space it takes on the system, and the subject.

The first message subject in the above list is in boldface, to let me know that I have not previously opened it. To open a message, click the subject line. Here is a message that I sent myself in Yahoo! Mail:

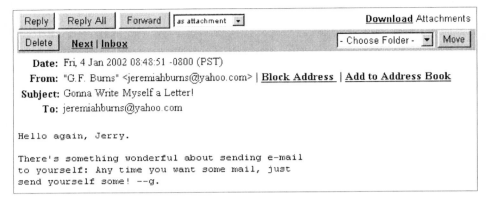

An open received message.

Replying to Mail

Open the message to which you want to reply.

Click **Reply** (or **Reply All**, if you want your reply to go to everyone addressed in the original message).

You'll see the **To** field completed with the sender's address, and **Re:** ("Regarding") preceding the original subject heading.

Place your cursor at the top of the message box and press the Enter key a couple of times to make a little space between your reply and the original message. When you have finished your reply, click Send. The system notifies you that your reply has been sent, and gives you choices about what to do with the original message, including moving to a different folder or deleting it.

Composing and Sending a Message

To write a message in Yahoo! Mail, click **Compose** in the left-hand menu of your email home page to go to the composition page.

Type a valid email address in the **To** field and a subject in the **Subject** field. Always use a subject header! Try to make it relevant to the content of the message. Messages without subject headers give the appearance of laziness on the part of the writer, and they are definitely rude—something like answering the telephone by saying "Yeah?"

Type your message in the message box. If you're brand-new to email, don't be concerned about the initial size of the box: If you type a long message, the system will automatically allow you to continue past the space that you first see in the message box. Here is another message that I just wrote to myself:

| Send | Save Draft | Spell Check | Cancel | |

Insert addresses from Address Book or enter nicknames (separated by commas)

To: `jeremiahburns@yahoo.com`

Subject: `Tired of Winter!`

Cc: `                          ` **Bcc:** `                          `

☐ **Send via free ZixMail.net*** What's this?   ☐ Save copy to Sent folder

Send an Invite or a Greeting Card

```
Hi, Jerry.

I'm not sure about this "Winter Wonderland" business.
If you ask me, 70 degrees year around woould work!

--Your frozen pal
```

Here is a message-in-progress with a problem.

Boy, somebody can't spell! Or maybe can't type. When you have finished your message, click **Spell Check** above the message headings. Not all free email systems offer a spell checker; Yahoo! is helpful that way. If the Yahoo! spell checker finds anything awry, it should alert you. The above message does have a misspelling. Clicking **Spell Check** on it produces this result:

Hi, Jerry.

I'm not sure about this "Winter Wonderland" business.

If you ask me, 70 degrees year around `woould` `?` work!

--Your frozen pal

| Done |

The spell checker spots the typo.

Isn't that nice? The system finds your typos and questionable spellings. There are two ways to repair these snags, once Yahoo! Mail has found them:

Click in the box with the error, enter the correct spelling, and click **Done**. Yahoo! Mail will return you to your composition, with the error repaired. If you would like suggestions from Yahoo! Mail on how to handle your error, click the question mark following the error. You will see suggested alternatives, from which you may select one that suits you. Then click **Done**, and you'll go back to your composition.

With your message written, spell-checked, and any errors corrected, click **Send** in the upper left corner above the message. (If you want to keep a copy of an email that you are going to send, click the check-box for **Save Copy to Sent Folder** before clicking **Send**.) Yahoo! Mail will give you instant feedback to let you know that it has sent your message, and will bounce you back to the Mail Home page.

Sending to Multiple Recipients

To send a message to more than one recipient, enter all the addresses in the **To (or Cc or Bcc)** field. Separate the addresses with commas.

Saving a Draft

Yahoo! Mail offers a handy way to save a draft of a message. There are any number of reasons to save a draft, but the two most basic are that you're working on a difficult message, and want to give it some time to simmer at the back of your mind before you finish and send it, or you're interrupted in the composition process by some external event. (Your spouse wants to go for a walk, the dog wants to go outdoors, your favorite television program is about to start, and so on.) To save a draft of your message in Yahoo! Mail, at any time during your composition click **Save Draft** at the top of the composition screen. The system will save the message on which you are working in the **Drafts** folder.

To return to your draft, click **Folders** in the menu, click **Draft**, and open your draft message by clicking on it.

Sending Copies

You can send copies of your message by entering addresses of the people you want to receive copies in the Cc ("carbon copy") or Bcc ("blind carbon copy") field. Remember that your primary recipient in the To field will not know that you have sent a copy of the message to anyone whose address you enter in the Bcc field. Potential trouble lies here. Please see the discussion of copies in this guide's first part.

Forwarding Mail

It is simple to forward a message that you have received to someone else, either as an attachment or as "inline text" (the forwarded message appears in the same message field as your supplementary comments).

To Forward a Message as an Attachment

With the message that you want to forward open, click the **Forward** button (next to the Reply All button). A message screen appears with the existing subject heading preceded by **Fwd:** ("Forward"). Like this:

Forwarding a message as an attachment.

Enter the email address of the person to whom you want to forward the message in the **To** field.

Add any introduction or commentary you wish to the message field.

Click **Send**

To Forward a Message as Inline Text

Select **inline text** by clicking on the pull-down menu to the right of the Forward button.

Click on *inline text* to forward the message in the message field of your outgoing message.

Click **inline text**

Click **Forward**

You will see the message screen open with the subject field already completed and the text of the original message in the message field. Place your cursor at the top of the message field; press Enter two or three times to separate your comments or introduction from the original message.

Add your comments above the message you are forwarding, and click **Send.**

Deleting Mail

To delete a message, with the message that you want to delete open, click **Delete.** The message will go into your Trash folder. Or,

Open any folder in which you have messages. Click the checkbox to the left of each message that you want to delete. (If you want to delete them all, click **Check All** at the left bottom of the list.)

Click **Delete.** The system will move all the messages into the Trash folder.

Yahoo! Mail automatically deletes the messages in your Trash folder from time to time. If you want to dump the trash earlier to conserve system space, click **Empty Trash** (just above the message list) in any folder.

Printing Mail

To print from Yahoo! Mail, click on **Printable View** near the top right corner of the message. This will simplify the format, and take less ink from your printer. After clicking Printable View, you may use the print function of your Web browser as you normally do.

Working with Folders

Folders are critical to efficient and orderly email handling. Yahoo! Mail provides four default folders: **Inbox, Sent, Draft,** and **Trash.** That is enough for elementary email, if you send and receive only a handful of messages now and then. If, like many email users, you find your email use growing at something like a geometric rate, you will definitely want to add more folders to your Yahoo! Mail. Otherwise, you will find yourself awash in messages from different people or organizations, on different topics, and for different purposes. If you're a frequent letter-to-the-editor writer, you'll find that the convenience of email was absolutely made to serve that habit. You will want separate folders for mail from your children or grandchildren, for your business, for clubs, hobbies, and so on. Placing email into folders specifically dedicated to the subjects (or sources) of the mail makes it far easier to find a message when you want it.

Creating a Folder

Click **Folders** on the Yahoo! Mail menu and you'll see this page (I have already added a "From the Kids" folder to my folder list):

Folder Name	Messages	Unread	Space Used	Create a personal folder
Inbox	5	1	18k	Folder name:
Draft	1	1	0k	Create folder
Sent	1	0	1k	
Trash [Empty]	1	0	22k	**Edit a personal folder:**
From the Kids	1	0	1k	Select a folder: From the Kids
TOTAL	**9**	**2**	**42k**	Rename Remove
				Only empty folders can be removed

A folder list with a newly made folder included.

On the right side of the screen, note the line **Create a personal folder**, and the box for the new **Folder name** just below it.

Type a name for the new folder in the box. Let's call this one "Home Business." Having typed in "Home Business" as the folder name, click **Create folder** just below the new name to add that folder to your folder list.

Saving Mail to a Folder

Let's open a message and move it into the Home Business folder. With the message open, click **Home Business** in the pull-down folder list at the upper right of the message:

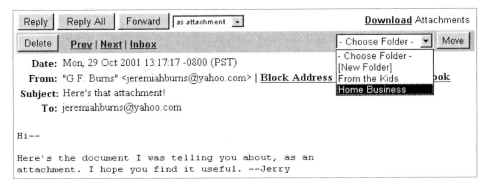

Click the *Move* button to place this message in the Home Business folder.

Click **Move** (just to the right of **Choose Folder**).

Yahoo! Mail will move the message to the Home Business folder.

Saving Mail on a Disk

You may use your usual Web browser function to save email to a floppy disk or to your computer's hard drive. It would be best to click on **Printable View** before saving a message; this will give you a simple, straightforward file.

Working with Attachments

An attachment is an already-existing computer file that you include with a message. It could be a word-processed document, an article or illustration that you downloaded from the Internet, a spreadsheet table, an audio clip, or something else that you want to share with your correspondent.

Creating an Attachment

Click **Add/Delete Attachments** at the bottom of an open message screen (notice that Yahoo! Mail has a new Add/Delete Video function, too):

☐ Use Signature ⦿ plain text ○ html tags allowed html preview	
Attachments: (None)	Add/Delete Attachments
Video: (None)	Add/Delete Video NEW!

Click *Add/Delete Attachments* below the message field.

After you click **Add/Delete Attachments**, you will see a pop-up window that includes this information:

Attachments   **Help**

Step 1: Click **Browse** and select a file.
If you do not see a "Browse" button, your browser does not support attachments.

Browse...

(PC users, select "All Files" for Files of Type.)

Step 2: Click **Attach File**.   Attach File

You may attach a maximum of three files. The total combined attachments may not exceed 1.5 megabytes.

Attached files	Size	Virus Check
No files attached		

Repeat steps 1 and 2 to attach more files.

Here's where you begin the attachment process in Yahoo! Mail.

Click **Browse** to select a file from your computer. Let's say that we want to send a file on a floppy disk in my A: drive.

As the illustration below indicates, I told the system to look in my A: drive, at a floppy disk with some old documents. I scrolled down in the Files of type box and selected All Files, so that I would see everything on the floppy disk listed on the screen. I want to send the file named "budget request" as an attachment.

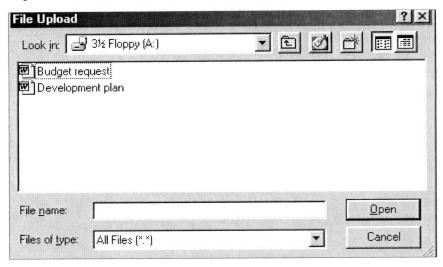

Selecting a file via browsing to send as an attachment.

Click the file name (in this case "budget request").

Click **Open**. Yahoo! Mail will return to the Attachments window, with the name and path of the selected file displayed.

Clicking the **Attach File** button in the next screen attaches the file to the email message.

One of Yahoo! Mail's most welcome attributes is its automatic scanning of outgoing attachments with the Norton AntiVirus program. Attachments are handy, but they are also notorious carriers of computer viruses. Yahoo! Mail's automatic virus scanning is a great way to help assure that you won't be sending your friends, business contacts, and other email recipients nasty bugs that will annoy them and their computers—or worse. Notice in the screen below the reassuring **No Threat Detected** in my attachment. That is what you want to see before you send an attachment with Yahoo! Mail.

Step 2: Click **Attach File**.   `Attach File`

You may attach a maximum of three files. The total combined attachments may not exceed 1.5 megabytes.

Attached files	Size	Virus Check
budget request.doc	33 K	No Threat Detected 🗑

Repeat steps 1 and 2 to attach more files.

It's good to see the "No Threat Detected" statement!

When you see the **No Threat Detected** line, click **Done**.

The system will return you to your message, with the name of the attached file appearing in the **Attachments** box. You may now finish your accompanying message, and click **Send**.

Scanning Incoming Attachments for Viruses

Yahoo! Mail also allows you to check incoming attachments for viruses. Even if your email correspondents are ordinarily careful not to send infected files, sometimes something might slip by them. It has happened to me, on both the receiving and sending ends. More than once I have discovered, shortly after sending an attachment to a friend, that the attachment concealed a virus. It's a little embarrassing to have to immediately send a new message with the header "Virus! Don't Open Previous Attachment!" Still, it happens to most of us, and the more you use attachments, the more likely it is that it will happen to you.

So you don't have to rely on your correspondents' caution, when you receive a message with an attachment in your Yahoo! Mail, click **Scan with Norton Antivirus** to be sure that your newly received attachment is bug-free. Yahoo! Mail recommends scanning the attachment that came with the email below (it's the budget request that I just sent to myself!).

Attachment	
📎 **budget_request.doc** **Type .doc** : Scanning recommended	**Scan With Norton Antivirus** **Download File** **View Attachment**

Yahoo! Mail encourages scanning this attachment.

When clicked **Scan with Norton Antivirus,** the system found that the attachment looked clean, as reported in the following screen:

Scan Result

Name of File: budget_request.doc

Type of File: application/msword

Scan Result: **No Virus Threat Detected**

| **Download Attachment** | **Back to Message** | **View Attachment** |

Disclaimer: This virus scanner may not be able to detect or repair all viruses and variants. Please be aware that there is a risk involved whenever downloading email attachments to your computer or sending email attachments to others and that, as provided in the Terms of Service, neither Yahoo nor its licensors are responsible for any damages caused by your decision to do so.

What a relief! This attachment is clean!

Notice the **disclaimer,** however. No vendor of a virus detecting and repair program would go far enough out on a limb to promise that there is a 100 percent certainty of a clean attachment. New viruses hit the Internet every day; virus hunters are continually tinkering with their programs so that they can be as confident as possible that they catch all the bad bugs. There are, however, no guarantees in life—or in computer virus detection, either. Nevertheless, the Norton Antivirus scan gives good reason to believe that this file is most likely not a danger, so...

Click **Download Attachment** to see and edit the file. To simply look at the file without downloading, click **View Attachment**. Keep in mind that you will need software on your computer able to open the attachment. Your email program itself does not open attachments for viewing or listening.

Working with the Address Book

The Yahoo! Mail address book allows you to store information, including email addresses, for up to 5,000 contacts, and permits creation of distribution lists so that you can easily send email to as many as 100 people at a time. You need to have contacts entered in your address book to make it work. Here's how:

To Add a Contact to Your Address Book

There are a variety of ways to add address book contacts, and the Yahoo! Mail Help function covers them all. For now, let's look at three basic methods:

In the Inbox, click on **Addresses** in the left-hand menu to open the address book.

Scroll down to the **Quick Add** module at the bottom of the address book:

Quick Add [Move To Top Of The Page]			
Last , First	Email	Phone	
	,		Work ▼	Add

The *Quick Add* module is at the bottom of the open Address Book.

Enter the information in the fields provided, and click **Add**.

Or, click the **New Contact** button at the top of the address book contacts page.

On the following page, enter the contact information for the person you wish to add.

Or, when you look at an incoming message, click **Add to Address Book** (immediately after **Block Address** in the **From** field).

Click the checkbox next to the address in the following screen:

Add Checked	Cancel			
Check All - Clear All				
Email Address	**First Name**	**Last Name**	**Nickname**	
☑ jeremiahburns@yahoo.com	G.F.	Burns		
Check All - Clear All				

Click the check box to the left of the name to select a contact for addition to the Address Book.

Click **Add Checked**

To Make a Distribution List

Click **Addresses** to open the address book.

Click **New List** near the top left of the Address Book page.

Enter the list name in the space provided. (Do *not* use spaces, commas, or single or double quotation marks. You can space words by using underscores, like this: City_Council_Group.) If you use forbidden characters in your list names, it will interfere with your ability to send mail.

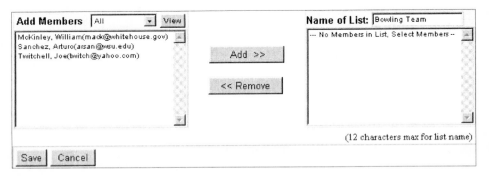

To add a member to the Bowling team list, click on a name in the *Add Members* box, then click the *Add* button.

Click on a contact from **Add Members** box on the left side of the screen.

Click **Add.** (You can add multiple contacts by holding down the **Ctrl** key on the keyboard as you select contacts.)

Click **Save** to save the list.

Sending Messages to Address Book Contacts

If you have not yet begun a message…

Click **Addresses** to open the address book.

Click on the email address of your intended recipient. A Compose Message window opens, with your selected contact's address in the **To** field. Proceed to write and send the message as usual.

If You Have Started a Message…

Click on the **To, Cc,** or **Bcc** links at the top of the Compose Mail window; the pop-up address book will appear.

Click to check the desired boxes (To, Cc, Bcc) beside your recipients' names; Or,

Click the **Distribution List** tab and click to check the desired lists.

Click **Done**. The system will return you to the Compose Mail window with the selected addresses in place. Write and send your message as usual.

Using Address Book Nicknames

Click **Compose** to open the Compose Mail screen.

Enter the nickname of your intended recipient in the To, Cc, or Bcc field. (You may also enter the name of a distribution list in these fields.)

Write and send your message as usual.

Sending a Message to Multiple Parties, or to a Distribution List

Click **Addresses** to open the address book.

Click on the boxes next to names of contacts or lists to which you want to send the message.

Click **Send Email** from the pull-down list on the right side of the page.

Click **Go**. A screen opens to confirm your selected recipients.

Click **Compose**. A screen will open with the selected address in the To field (or in the Cc or Bcc field, if that was your choice).

Compose and send your message as usual.

Some Other Yahoo! Mail Features

Yahoo! Mail offers a variety of services that can make emailing easier for you, and for those with whom you exchange messages. Clicking on the **Options** link on the menu produces a page which gives concise descriptions of available "extras." Yahoo! Mail offers most of these extras at no charge. The options include creation of a signature; an automatic Vacation Response that lets people know when you're away if they send you messages; POP3 mail client access and forwarding; and filters to sort incoming mail into specified folders.

One agreeable feature is Yahoo! Mail's spam detection system. This system identifies bulk email (also known as spam) and directs it to your Bulk Mail folder, rather than your Inbox

Search

The more email you have in your folders, the more useful the search feature can be. No matter how tidy your folder housekeeping, you will inevitably need to find a message, but will not be able to remember where you probably put it. The search feature will help you find it.

Mail Add-Ons

These premium features, available for a fee, range from extra system storage space (handy if you send and receive lots of mail, and want to save large chunks of it on the system), to registering your own Web address and having your Website hosted by Yahoo! GeoCities.

Help Function

The Yahoo! Mail help system keys to the function that you're presently using, e.g., composing messages or using folders. To enter the help system from any point in Yahoo! Mail, click **Help** in the upper-right corner of the screen. In addition to basic help, including answers to FAQs (Frequently Asked Questions), Yahoo! Mail help allows you to send questions online directly to Yahoo! staff.

PART THREE

Standalone Systems

EUDORA

QUALCOMM's standalone Eudora system is a very nice free downloadable program. Do not confuse it with Eudora WebMail. This Eudora is not only from a different vendor; it installs on your computer. You are not going to use it at the public library or in a cybercafe, as you might Eudora WebMail. It is not, then, a "portable" system, but it packs more power than Web mail systems.

Obtaining Eudora

Go to the following Web site: *http://www.eudora.com*

The full-featured program, Eudora Version 5.1, is available at no charge. Eudora does have a "light" version, but why not go for the whole package? You may never use all the features, but it's nice to know that they're at your service if you need them. It's hard to argue with the price, too. In this overview, we'll look at the basic functions of the program, and not stray too far into the system's nifty extras. Eudora's Help function covers all the extras, however, so as well as having them, you can find out how to use them.

If you download the full-featured free version of Eudora 5.1, you will see ads on the screen, as you do in free Web mail. Eudora promises "to present the ads in a way that respects the work you do in email." After a trial period in the free full version, Eudora will ask you to provide profile information. You'll need to do that to enjoy continued use of the full free package.

If you're disinclined to profile yourself for advertising purposes, or simply cannot stand even unobtrusive ads, Eudora gives you two options: You can pay for the ad-free full version ($39.95, at this date), or you can download the "Light Mode." Although it has fewer features, Eudora Light includes no ads. The choice is yours. Whichever choice you make, chances are good that you will find this a satisfying program.

Because Eudora is a richly endowed program, with far more features than you are likely to master overnight, it would be helpful to explore its capabilities and functions slowly. It will not take long at all to learn the most basic emailing routines, but when the menu of possibilities is as full as Eudora's, it is probably better to sample the advanced items one at a time, rather than trying to swallow the whole array in one gulp.

When you download Eudora, save it in a folder on your computer that you have designated "Downloads." If you have not yet done so, you will find it very helpful to keep programs that you download in a separate folder. It will save you time trying to find them if they are scattered around in your computer.

After saving Eudora 5.1 to your download folder, open that folder and click on the Eudora icon to start the installation. Follow the on-screen directions. As with other downloadable email programs, when you install Eudora you will need to have an email address, a system password, and the names of your incoming POP3 (Post Office Protocol), IMAP, or HTTP protocols, and your outgoing SMTP (Simple Mail Transfer Protocol) server. If you do not know these details, your Internet Service Provider will be able to tell you.

Retrieving Messages in Eudora 5.1

Open Eudora from Windows. You can open it from the taskbar, or by clicking **Start**, pointing to **Programs**, and clicking on Eudora from the subsequent program list. If you have set up a desktop icon for Eudora, you can click on the icon to open the program.

At the **Mailbox** menu, click **In**. You will see messages listed in reverse chronological order—the oldest ones first. Any messages that you have not opened will show a bullet in the Status column, like this:

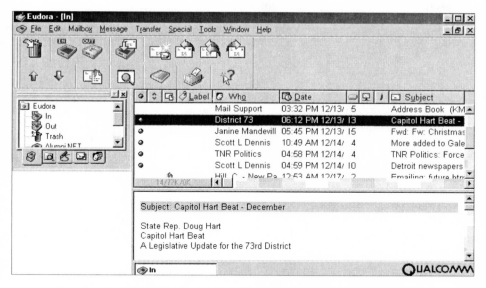

Unopened messages marked with bullets. (Source: QUALCOMM, Inc.)

To open a message, double-click its summary. When a message summary is highlighted, you may also read the message in the preview window below the mailbox. (You can expand or reduce the height of the preview window by clicking on the bar separating it from the message list and dragging it up or down. You can also cancel the Preview Pane entirely in the Tools/Options menu.)

To close a message, click on the lower X in the upper right corner of the screen.

You may retain messages indefinitely in your Eudora 5.1 mailbox. It will be helpful for organizational purposes if you move messages of related kinds to other mailboxes that you create. Many email users negligent about setting up mailboxes and moving their messages to them have found themselves with hundreds of messages in their inboxes. The longer you go without tending to the housekeeping of your mailboxes, the more tedious it will be when you finally get around to it. We'll have more to say about creating mailboxes later.

New Mail Alerts

Eudora will alert you to newly received mail in a number of ways: through an alert dialog box; by opening the mailbox (your inbox, unless you have set up filters to direct mail elsewhere); and by making a "New Mail" sound. You control these actions in the **Getting Attention** window. To do it:

Click **Tools**

Click **Options**

Scroll to and click **Getting Attention**

Make your choices.

Replying to Messages in Eudora 5.1

You may respond to messages in different ways. The easiest and most straightforward:

Click the **Reply** icon on the toolbar. The Reply to Sender icon is the one with the single arrow pointing to the left; Reply to All (if you want everyone addressed in the original To field to see your response) is the one next to it, with two arrows pointing left.

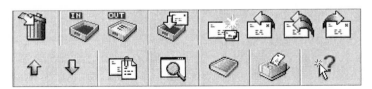

The Eudora 5.1 toolbar. (Source: QUALCOMM, Inc.)

When you click Reply, the system automatically enters the address in the To field, your address in the From field, and the subject, preceded by "Re:" ("Regarding"), like this:

To: "Chuptoss, Clyde" <chuptoss@uksask.edu>
From: Grant Burns <gfburns@quark.edu>
Subject: RE: NCA
Cc:
Bcc:
Attached:

Information automatically added to headers after clicking on the *Reply* button. (Source: QUALCOMM, Inc.)

To keep a copy of your reply, hold down the shift key on your keyboard while you click Reply. Type your message in the message field, above the original message.

Click **Send**

Composing and Sending a Message

Click the **New Message** button at the top center of the In box toolbar (to the immediate left of the Reply button)

Enter a valid email address (or addresses) in the **To** field.

Enter a word or phrase in the **Subject** field that reasonably characterizes the content of your message. Take the time to think of a good subject heading; good subject headings not only make it easier for your recipients to grasp quickly the topics of your messages; they also make it much easier for you to keep your messages organized and to retrieve specific messages without difficulty.

Type your message in the message body.

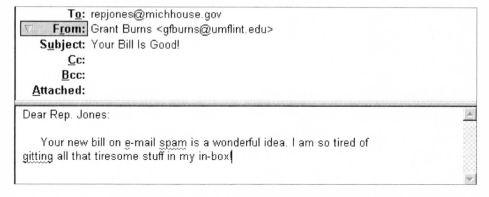

To: repjones@michhouse.gov
From: Grant Burns <gfburns@umflint.edu>
Subject: Your Bill Is Good!
Cc:
Bcc:
Attached:

Dear Rep. Jones:

Your new bill on e-mail spam is a wonderful idea. I am so tired of gitting all that tiresome stuff in my in-box

A quick (too-quick) note of thanks to my state representative. (Source: QUALCOMM, Inc.)

When you are through typing, it would be a good idea to spell check. Eudora can be set to spell check automatically (read the Help function!); you can also spell check manually very easily:

With the message open, click **Edit**

Click **Check Spelling** in the pull-down Edit menu

The **Check Spelling** window opens. Eudora identifies questionable spellings, and gives you options for changing them. You may click on a selection from the scroll-down list, or delete the word in the **Change to:** box and type in another word. Eudora found my error in the above message:

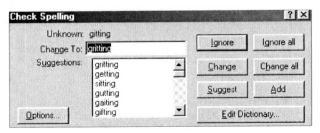

To correct my typo, I'll click on the correct spelling, then click *Change.* (Source: QUALCOMM, Inc.)

Eudora will make the changes you indicate. When you are through spell checking, Eudora will return you to the message.

Click **Send**

What happens then? If you have Eudora set to send messages immediately (the Immediate Send option in the **Sending Mail Options Window** is on), and you are online, the message will go off to its recipient. You can also have the message set aside in a queuing file to send later. To make such choices, you need to become acquainted with the Options function:

Click **Tools** at the top of the screen.

Click **Options** at the bottom of the Tools menu. You will see a long list of categories beginning with these functions:

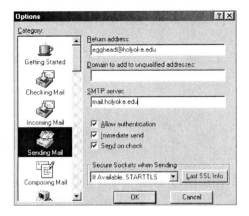

The opening items in the Categories. We're at the *Sending Mail* options on the right. (Source: QUALCOMM, Inc.)

Click on any of the functions to see choices that you can make on how you want the system to handle your mail. Above, I clicked on Sending Mail.

To Cancel a Message that You Have Begun

Click **File**

Click **Close**

Click **No** in the **Save Changes** box

Some Formatting Notes

Eudora 5.1 includes many advanced formatting options, including the ability to boldface your type, to underline, strikeout, align left, right, or center, and so on. If you know that you are sending a message to someone whose email system supports these formatting fine points, go ahead and use them. If you do not know whether your recipient's system has that ability, go easy on the elaborate formatting: It might not come through well at all. Your safest bet in this case is to send your message with as little formatting finery as possible, even to the point of using such email conventions as asterisks for emphasis and partial underscoring (e.g., _Moby Dick_) to indicate italics or more complete underscoring.

Saving Copies of Outgoing Messages

Ordinarily, you will at least initially save copies of messages that you send in your Out mailbox. (You may decide to move them to other mailboxes or folders later.) To keep a copy of every message you send in your Out mailbox:

In the **Composing Mail Options** window, turn on the **Keep copies** option:

Click **Tools**

Click **Options**

Click **Composing Mail** in the **Category** window

Click the **Keep Copies** checkbox

If you have not set the keep copies option but want to keep a copy of a specific message:

Click **Keep Copy** in the message toolbar (just above the "TT" symbol midway across the toolbar).

To place a copy of a message that you are sending in a specific mailbox other than the Out box, right-click in the body of the message. Select the mailbox from the Fcc menu.

Eudora 5.1 allows great flexibility in saving sent messages. In addition to the above methods, you may set the system to save messages in specific mailboxes according to information in the messages. This procedure is beyond the scope of a basic how-to, but the Eudora 5.1 Help function will walk you through it in good form.

Sending to Multiple Recipients

Use commas to separate multiple addresses in the To, Cc, or Bcc fields.

Saving a Draft of a Message

If you are working on a difficult message, or one that requires checking details elsewhere before you send it, or you simply want to take a walk around the block and get some air before resuming, you can easily save your message in progress and return to it later.

Click on the **File** menu.

Click **Save**

Eudora saves the message in the Out mailbox, from which you can retrieve it when ready. You can now either close the message, or work further on it. Eudora will help you avoid losing work by asking you, when you try to close a message that you have not saved, if you want to save it.

Retrieving a Draft

Double click the Out mailbox icon in your Mailbox window on the left side of the screen.

In the message list, double click the summary of the message you want to retrieve.

Sending Copies

If you would like to send copies of a message, use the **Cc** or **Bcc** fields, or both. Everyone who receives the message will see all the addresses in the Cc field, but addresses entered in the Bcc field will not be visible to anyone whose address is in the To or Cc field. There are social and political issues involved in sending copies, particularly blind copies. Please see the discussion of copies in this guide's first part.

You may also use the Bcc field to send a copy of the message to any of your mailboxes. To do so:

Right-click in the message body.

Choose a mailbox from the **Fcc** ("Folder carbon copy") menu. The mailbox name goes into the Bcc field.

When you send the message, the blind copy goes to the mailbox you designated.

Forwarding Messages

It is easy to forward to someone else a message that you have received. To do it:

In a message list, click on the message you would like to forward.

Click **Forward** on the Message menu.

You will see a new message window with your address in the From field and the original subject header, preceded by **Fwd:**, in the Subject field.

Enter your intended recipient's email address in the To field.

Above the original message in the message body, type your introduction or commentary. You need not be wordy here, but it is usually helpful for the recipient of a forwarding to receive a little orientation to the forwarded message.

Click **Send**

Eudora 5.1 provides other ways to forward messages; the above method is the easiest. Eudora's very detailed Help function covers the others.

Deleting Messages

Like many other email systems, Eudora 5.1 uses a two-step procedure for message deletion. This two-step procedure is not the result of clumsiness, but of an interest in helping you avoid inadvertent deletion of a message. Having used systems that employed a one-step deletion process—delete it and it's gone forever—I can testify to the value of this safeguard process. Realizing a moment after deleting a message that it was one you really needed is not a pleasant experience.

To Delete a Message If You Have POP Email

Click on the message you want to delete

From the Message menu, click **Delete** (or **Trash** from the Transfer menu, or press the **Delete** key on your keyboard, or click the **Delete** toolbar button). The message will go to the Trash mailbox. (You can cancel this deletion, if you wish: Click the **Edit** menu, and click **Undo**.)

To Remove Messages from the Trash Mailbox

Click on the **Special** menu at the top of the screen.

Click **Empty Trash** in the Special menu.

Alternatively:

In the open **Mailboxes** window, on the left side of the screen (it looks like this:)

The Trash folder selected in the Folder tree. (Source: QUALCOMM, Inc.)

Right-click the **Trash** mailbox and click **Empty Trash** in the pull-down menu.

Turn on the **Empty Trash when exiting** option in the **Miscellaneous options** window. (Click the **Tools** menu; click **Options**; click **Miscellaneous** options). With this option in place, Eudora will empty the Trash whenever you quit the program;

Or, to delete messages selectively from Eudora's Trash:

Open the Trash mailbox.

Select the messages you want to eliminate.

Press the **Delete** key on your keyboard (or click **Delete** in the Message menu).

To Delete a Message If You Have IMAP Email

Eudora notes that if you turn off the incoming mail option that directs the system to move a deleted message to Trash, you must follow a two-step deletion process:

Mark the message for deletion by selecting it.

From the Message menu, click **Delete**, or press the Delete key.

To remove all marked messages, choose Purge Messages from the Message menu. Be careful: the Purge Messages function does what it says: When a message has been purged, it is gone for good.

Printing Messages

Click **File** in the upper left corner of the screen.

Click **Print**

Follow the usual routine with your printer.

Working with Folders and Mailboxes

Eudora offers a very nice folder and mailbox system. Your default setup consists of three mailboxes: **In, Out** (i.e., your sent mail), and **Trash**, in a single folder. You will almost certainly want to create more mailboxes, and more folders, to manage your mail, especially if you send and receive a lot of it. Taking the time for effective folder and mailbox management will pay you back many times over in the time you save hunting for messages that you "know" you have somewhere, if only you could find them.

Creating a Mailbox or Mail Folder

When you open Eudora, you'll see your folders and mailboxes in a "tree" arrangement in the small window on the left side of the screen. It will be a very simple tree at first, with your default mailboxes lined up under the Eudora folder. In Eudora, **Mailboxes** are the places you put your mail; **Folders** are the places where you put your mailboxes. You might, for example, have a folder named "Work Mail," and in your Work Mail folder have a separate mailbox for each person at work with whom you exchange email. It will be far easier for you to find the important message that Joe in Accounting sent you last month if you save it systematically, like this, rather than letting it sit forever with hundreds of other messages in your In box.

Let's create a new mailbox, and a folder to keep it in:

Make sure your Mailbox and Folder tree is visible in the window on the left. You should see the "Eudora" folder, and below it the In, Out, and Trash mailboxes. If you do not see them, click the far-left ("Mailboxes") tab below the left window. Your tree structure will appear. Here is my tree structure, at the moment:

Click the first button at the bottom left if you do not see your Folder tree in this box. (Source: QUALCOMM, Inc.)

Right-click on the "Eudora" folder at the top of the window. You will see a pop-up menu.

Click **New** in the pop-up menu. This will open a dialog box, like this:

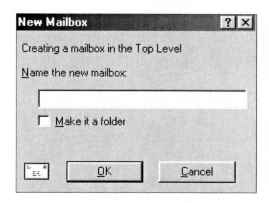

To create a new mailbox, enter its name and click *OK*. (Source: QUALCOMM, Inc.)

Type the name of your new folder in the dialog box.

Click the checkbox in front of **Make it a folder**. I am making a folder that we'll call "Favorite Sports."

Click **OK**. This will establish your folder, and open another dialog box, like this:

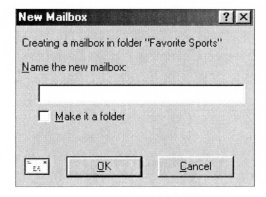

I need to make a mailbox to go into my new folder. (Source: QUALCOMM, Inc.)

Type in the name of your new mailbox that will be contained in the folder you just made. (I'm going to make a mailbox for "Table Tennis.")

Click **OK**

You will see in the tree structure in the Mailbox window the new folder name, and the mailbox below it and indented to indicate that it is within that folder.

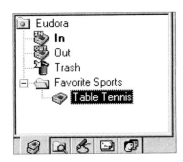

The "Table Tennis" mailbox now appears in the Folder tree, contained in the folder "Favorite Sports." (Source: QUALCOMM, Inc.)

You can add additional mailboxes to a folder:

Right-click on the folder where you want to add a mailbox.

Click **New** in the pop-up menu.

Type the new mailbox name into the dialog box.

Click **OK**

To condense the tree structure in your Mailbox window, click on the minus (-) sign before each folder. To open up the tree structure so that you can see all the mailboxes in a folder, click the plus (+) sign before a folder.

Saving (Transferring) Messages to a Mailbox

You can transfer a message to any mailbox in Eudora.

One way to do it:

Click on the message in a message list.

Click **Transfer** at the top of the toolbar to open the pull-down menu.

Click on the mailbox where you want to save the message.

Another way to do it:

Click on the message.

Right-click the selected message.

Click on a mailbox in the Transfer submenu.

The easiest way to do it:

Click on a message summary in a message list and hold down the left mouse button while you drag the summary and drop it on a mailbox icon in the Mailboxes window.

Saving Messages to a File

You may want to save a message in another file on your computer or on a floppy disk, rather than in Eudora. Here's how:

Open or select the message you want to save.

Click the **File** menu.

Click **Save As**

In the Save As dialog box, type in the name you want to assign the file and choose the desired options. Here I am saving the message "Handicapped Study Room" on a floppy disk in my A: drive.

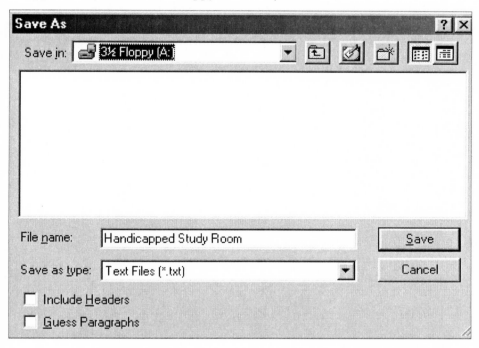

Saving a message to a floppy disk in the A: drive. (Source: QUALCOMM, Inc.)

If you check **Include Headers**, the header of the first message in the file to be saved will be included. If you do not check Include Headers, the system will save only the body of the message (or messages, if there is more than one).

If you check **Guess Paragraphs**, the system will remove extra Enter-key "returns" from the message, leaving them only at the ends of paragraphs; it will also change multiple spaces to tabs.

The **Save as type** option should be **Text Files**.

When you have finished, click **Save** in the dialog box.

Working with Attachments

Attachments are previously existing computer files that can be included with email messages. These files may be sound files, documents from a word processing program, pictures, spreadsheets, or other kinds of files. Attachments are very useful for transferring electronic content quickly and efficiently. They also provide, unfortunately, the reigning favorite medium for the transmission of computer viruses. Because malicious people use attachments so often for the perverse sport of doing everything from bogging down Internet traffic to ruining the work of computer users they have never met, everyone who uses attachments must take care not to send virus-infected attachments to others, or to open them after receiving them. As a prevailing rule, it is by opening infected attachments that one's own computer becomes infected. (There are other means of virus infection, but attachments are the prime carriers.)

Eudora 5.1 emailers should use their own virus scanning and repair programs, such as McAfee VirusScan, to be sure that both the attachments they send and the ones they have received and plan to open are clean. Sending and opening attachments without scanning for viruses is not responsible emailing. If you receive an attachment, open the message with the attachment, save the message to a floppy disk or to a folder in your hard drive following the normal procedure with your browser, then scan it.

Making and Sending an Attachment

Start a new message.

Click the **Message** menu at the top of the screen to open a long pull-down menu:

Click *Attach File* on the message menu. (Source: QUALCOMM, Inc.)

Click **Attach File**

You will see the **Attach File** dialog box.

Find the file you want to attach. Here I have scrolled down to my A: drive in the **Look in:** box, and have clicked on a file, "UF no. 6."

Double-click the file, or click **Attach**. The attachment will be indicated in the **Attached** field in the message headers, like this:

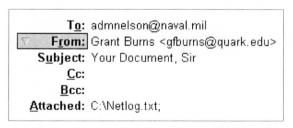

In the message headers, the last one indicates your outgoing attachment. (Source: QUALCOMM, Inc.)

You may add multiple attachments to a message by using the above procedure. You may, if you wish, attach files to a message by dragging them from the Desktop or the File Browser window onto the message window.

Complete your message and click **Send**.

Receiving and Opening an Attachment

When you receive an attachment, Eudora automatically decodes it and saves it. You will see attachment names at the bottom of incoming messages and in the message preview window:

You will see attachments indicated with a symbol like this at the bottom of an incoming message. (Source: QUALCOMM, Inc.)

After scanning the message for viruses, you can open an attachment in either an open message or the message preview window. Click on the attachment name or the attachment icon. The attachment will open, assuming that your computer has a program that can handle it. For example, if a friend sends you an attached document composed in Microsoft Word, and you have Word on your computer, it should open the attachment when you click on it.

Do not open any attachment unless you are confident that it is virus-free!

Working with the Address Book

Maintaining an address book of your email contacts, both individuals and groups, makes it easier to send messages. Instead of banging away at lengthy and easily-bungled email addresses, you can use the Eudora Address Book to address messages quickly and easily. Before you can use the Address Book, you must put some entries into it!

Adding Someone to the Address Book

Click the **Address Book** icon on the toolbar (just below the New Message icon)

Click **New** in the Address Book to prepare the Address Book for your new entry. Here I have already entered several nicknames, including one group nickname, in my Address Book:

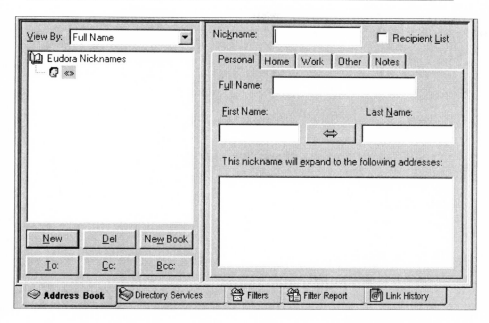

Add Address Book entries for individuals in this box. (Source: QUALCOMM, Inc.)

In the **Nickname** field on the right, type the name you want to assign your contact. You will be able to use nicknames from the Address Book when addressing messages, rather than entering full email addresses in the To, Cc, or Bcc fields. The nickname could be a single name (Jim, Mary, Rover), or a genuine nickname (Skippy, Gonzo, Whitey), or a formal name (John Brown, Jane Addams). Do *not* use an actual email address as a nickname. That won't work. It probably would not occur to you to use an actual email address as a nickname, but people do some strange things with email, and someone has probably tried to do this.

To place the name on your Quick Recipient list (your frequent email contacts):

Check the **Recipient List** box.

Press the **Enter** key, or click anywhere. Eudora will establish the entry.

Click the **Personal** tab, if that is not the open tab window.

In the full name field, enter your contact's name.

Enter the first and last names in the designated boxes. If you happen to put the first name in the Last Name box, and vice versa, it's easy to fix: Just click the "swap" arrow between the names, and they'll swap places.

Enter the full email address of your contact in the field headed **This nickname will expand...** (You may enter additional email addresses for this individual in this space, but do not add anything else.)

If you wish, click the remaining tabs to enter further information on this contact.

All done? Click **File**, then click **Save**.

Making a Distribution List

If you send messages to groups, you will appreciate the way Eudora facilitates the task of addressing. Let's make a list:

Click the **Address Book** icon on the toolbar.

If you have more than one address book, click on the one in which one you want to put your new list (or group, as Eudora calls it).

Click **New**
Enter the group nickname.

Press the **Enter** key or click anywhere. The nickname will display in the list.

Click the **Personal** tab.

Enter a name for the group in the **Full Name** field.

Type the complete email address for each person in the group in the **This nickname will expand...** field. At the end of each address, either type a comma or press the Enter key. You *can* enter nicknames here, provided you have already set up entries for them in the Address Book. Don't type anything else in this field except complete email addresses and the commas to separate them.

To add the group to your recipient list, click the **Recipient List** box.

Done? Click **File**, then click **Save**.

Sending a Message from the Address Book

Click the **Address Book** icon on the toolbar.

Click on the entry for the contact or group to whom you want to send a message. (You can select consecutive entries if you hold down the Shift key, or nonconsecutive entries by pressing the Ctrl key.)

Click the **To**, **Cc**, or **Bcc** button at the bottom of the Address Book box. Eudora places any nickname selected in the chosen field in a new message screen. I clicked on Eddie here, held down the Ctrl key, and clicked on Jerry:

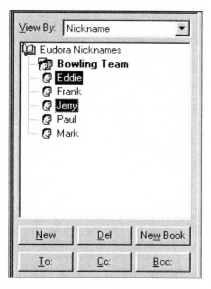

To select multiple nicknames, press and hold *Ctrl* while clicking on your selections. (Source: QUALCOMM, Inc.)

Enter a subject and complete and send your message as usual.

Battling Spam with Filters

Eudora allows a considerable range of "filtering" functions to help you manage your email. The system Help function covers them in detail. One that you should be aware of at the outset is how to use Eudora's filter function to fight spam. If you receive any spam, here is a quick way to deal with it, and with subsequent spams from the same source:

Right-click in the body of the open message, or on the message summary in your In box.

Click **Make Filter** from the pull-down menu. The **Make a Filter** dialog box will appear. This box allows you to make choices to determine how messages on a particular subject or from a specific source will be handled in the future. If you're dealing with spam, in the **Match Conditions** area of the dialog box, you will:

Click **Incoming**

Click **From**

In the **Action** area of the dialog box, you will click **Delete Message**. This will send further incoming messages from the specified sender, or on the specified subject, straight to your Trash Mailbox.

Click **Create Filter**. If I click Create Filter in the following Make Filter box, future messages from Edgar Montrose will go into my Trash folder.

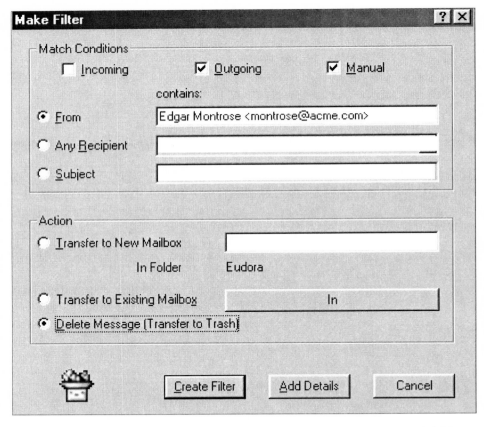

To avoid hearing from Edgar, I'll have Eudora filter his messages into my Trash folder. (Source: QUALCOMM, Inc.)

There. As long as the spammer is not creative enough to change his "From" identification, if you selected the From match, you should see his pitches only in your Trash Mailbox.

Eudora 5.1 is rich with features accessible through click-on buttons and drop-down menus. They include such functions as "Return Receipt" (which leads to your notification when a recipient opens a message you sent); signature management; text color; alignment; underlining and italics, and many others. One of Eudora's most striking "extras" is the Mood Watch option. If activated (click Tools; click Options; scroll to and click the Mood Watch icon), Eudora will alert you to messages both from others and that you compose yourself that may have offensive content. Eudora provides this alert in the form of one to three chili pepper symbols, depending on the message's combustible qualities.

Eudora also features an Extra Warnings function in the Options window. Here, you can instruct the system to alert you if you try to do something out-of-bounds, such as deleting unread mail, or launching a program from a message without scanning for viruses. Eudora 5.1 tries hard to keep its users on the straight and narrow!

I have covered only the most basic of Eudora 5.1's features here, enough to get you started sending, receiving, and filing your email. You will find that there is often more than one way to operate a particular function in the system; in this introduction I tried to highlight the most straightforward of those functions. Eudora 5.1 is an excellent choice for the serious emailer who is willing to spend enough time with the system's detailed Help function to learn how to make the program stand up and do its tricks. Casual emailers can use it for basic work, of course, without concerning themselves about all the system's bells and whistles. You will find that if you investigate Eudora's Help function (there is both an indexed section and a searchable section), you will discover a wide array of useful options, with clear instructions for putting them into effect.

JUNO

Juno is an interesting and unusual entry in the free email arena. Although the program downloads to your computer, rather than existing "out there" on the Web, it does not require you to connect through a separate Internet Service Provider. Juno itself supplies an Internet connection as part of its free package. At this date, Juno has over 2,000 dial-in numbers across the United States to support its users' Internet and Web access.

Like most free Web-based email programs, Juno maintains its free access through online advertising. (Juno offers a modestly-priced premium service for those who want to avoid the ads). Whether one opts for the free Juno or a premium package, the system is a nice alternative to the prevailing ISP/Web-mail/client-based email configurations. If you live in a community of reasonably substantial size, chances are that Juno can offer you a local telephone number to support your dial-up access.

Downloading Juno to Your Computer

To download Juno, you need a Microsoft Windows operating system (95 and up), at least a 14.4K modem (56K would be better; as with speakers for your stereo system, this is one place where you don't want to play it cheap with the idea that you're doing yourself a favor), and a number of other system capabilities. If your computer was new within the past few years, it is probably ready to roll, with the possible exception of the modem.

Go to *http://www.juno.com*

Juno gives you clear instructions when you click **Downloading** at the Juno home page. Clear instructions, in fact, are a Juno hallmark; it is obvious that some people took considerable care in making Juno procedures comprehensible to those who can read, but who are not, dare we use the term, "computer literate."

Creating a New Account

When you have downloaded and installed Juno on your computer according to the system's directions, start the program. You will see first the **Welcome to Juno** box.

Click **Create Account** on the right side of the box. Juno will systematically walk you through the connections setup, email address, dial-in number, and so on. It is a straightforward, easy procedure. You will, of course, have to click on a statement indicating that you accept Juno's terms of service if you are to proceed with the program.

Composing and Sending a Message

You do not need to be connected to the Internet to compose a message in Juno.

Click on the **Write** tab (top left of screen) in any folder. You will see the Write screen open.

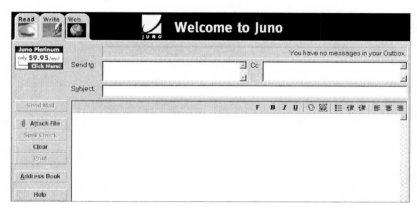

Juno's Write screen.

Type a valid email address in the **Send to** field. Press the Tab key to move the cursor to the **Subject** field.

Type the subject of your message in the **Subject** field. Tab again to move the cursor to the beginning of the message field.

When you finish typing your message, click **Spell Check** in the left margin. If Juno's spell-checker finds a questionable spelling, it will alert you with a box like this:

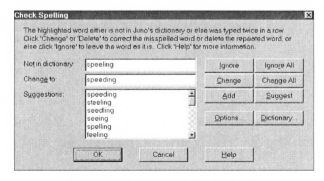

Juno's spell checker suggests a correction.

I deliberately misspelled "spelling" in my message; Juno caught the error. To correct it, I'll click on the correct spelling in the **Suggestions** list, and click **Change** to correct the spelling.

At this point, Juno offers several choices. You can:

- Save the message as a Draft

- Send the message

- Put the message in your Outbox

To Save a Draft

At the message you are writing:

Click **File**

Click **Save Message as Draft**

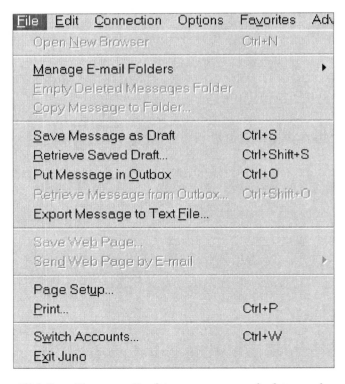

Click *Save Message as Draft* to save a message for later work.

Click **OK** when you see the confirmation that your draft has been saved.

To Retrieve a Draft

Click **File**

Click **Retrieve Saved Draft**
Click on the message summary in the "Retrieve Saved Draft" box.

Click the **Retrieve** button at the bottom of the "Retrieve Saved Draft" box.
The saved message will open so that you can continue working on it.

To Send the Message

Click **Send Mail** on the left margin. This action will dial up Juno's central computers through your modem, and send your message. Once you have dialed into the system, you will also be able to retrieve your new email, if there is any. But wait…

If you plan to send more than one message during this session, Juno advises you to put your ready-to-send message into your **Outbox**. There it, and others to follow, will stay until you click Send Mail. Then Juno will send all the messages in your Outbox. This will make your emailing much more efficient, and could cut down on your phone bill: no need to connect to the Internet a half-dozen or more times to send a series of messages. One connection (one phone call), and they're all off to their recipients.

To Put a Message into the Outbox

With the message open, click **File**.

Click **Put Message in Outbox**

Sending to Multiple Recipients

Separate multiple addresses in the **Send To** field with commas.

Clearing a Message in the Write Page

If you're working on a message and decide you want to start over—or simply forget it altogether—click **Clear** in the left margin. The message disappears.

Sending Copies

Type a valid email address in the Cc ("carbon copy") field.

To send a blind copy (one that your primary recipient is unaware that you sent), enclose the address in the Cc field in parentheses. If you want to send multiple blind copies, enter the addresses (separated by commas) and enclose the entire group with parentheses. You may, if you wish, enclose each address with parentheses.

Forwarding a Message

If you would like to send a message that you received to someone else, open the message, or click on it in the message list in a folder.

Click **Forward** in the left margin. The system will put an Fw: before the message's Subject field, and will include the forwarded message in the message field.

Type the email address of the person to whom you want to forward the message in the Send To field.

You will probably want to include some commentary of your own; forwarded messages are much easier to make sense of with some orienting verbiage, even if no more than "fyi" ("for your information"). Place your cursor above the original message in the message field; press the Enter key a few times to open some space between your added comments and the message to be forwarded. Write your introduction to the forwarding, and click Send Mail.

To Retrieve a Message

Click the **Read** tab.

Click the arrow on the pull-down **Folder** menu if the message you want is in a folder other than the one presently open.

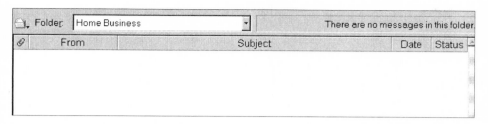

Note the pull-down **Folder** menu at the top of the screen in the Juno *Read* function.

Click the message line in the message list to see the message.

To Reply to a Message

With the message open, click **Reply**. The **Reply Settings** box opens.

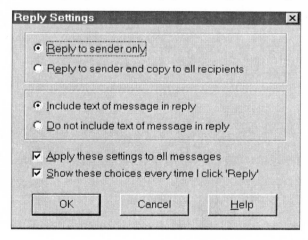

Juno's *Reply Settings* box.

Click the check boxes to choose your preferences.

Click **OK**

If you retain the text of the original message, with your cursor above the message in the message field, press the Enter key a few times to open some space between your message and the original.

Type your message.

Click **Spell Check** and follow through on that procedure, as described above.

Click **Send Mail** (or click File, and click Put Message in Outbox for later sending).

(If you change your mind and click **Clear** here, you delete only the reply-in-progress, not the original message. That remains in the folder it was in when you began the reply.)

Deleting Messages

What you do to delete messages in Juno depends on where you are in the system.

In the **Read** function:

In the message list, click on the message you want to delete.

Click **Delete** on the left side of the screen.

Click **Yes** if you see a confirmation message. The message will go into your Deleted Messages folder.

In the **Outbox:**

Click **File**

Click **Retrieve Message from Outbox**
Click on the pertinent message in the message list.

Click **Delete**

Click **Yes** if you see a confirmation message. The deleted messages goes into your Deleted Messages folder.

In the **Write** function:

Click **Clear** to delete the message. Messages that you clear are completely gone. They do not go into the Deleted Messages folder.

Deleting a Saved Draft

Click **File**

Click **Retrieve Saved Draft**
Click the pertinent message in the message list.

Click **Delete**

Click **Yes** if a confirmation message appears. The message goes into the Deleted Messages folder.

What Happens to Messages in the Deleted Messages Folder?

Unless you disable the function, Juno automatically empties your Deleted Messages folder when you exit your account.

Printing Messages

In the **Write** function:

Click **Print** in the left-hand menu.

In the **Print** dialog box, select the appropriate settings.

Click **OK**

In the **Read** function:

Click the message to be printed.

Click **Print**

Select the appropriate settings in the **Print** dialog box.

Click **OK**

Working with Folders

An email folder is a place where messages exist. Every email system comes with some default folders; Juno's are the **Inbox, Sent Messages, Draft,** and **Deleted Messages.** You will soon find it helpful to add new folders so that you can organize your messages by subject or by sender. Leaving all your incoming mail in your Inbox is a sure ticket to confusion. Juno allows up to 253 folders, in addition to the default group. That should be enough to satisfy even the most dedicated email organizer.

Creating a Folder

Click **File**

Place the pointer on **Manage Email Folders.**

Click **Create Folder**. You will see the Create Folder dialog box.

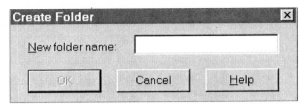

The *Create Folder* dialog box.

Type a name for the new folder in the **New Folder** name box.

Click **OK**

Saving a Message in a Folder

In a message list, click the message you plan to move to the folder.
Click **Move to Folder** in the left-hand menu.
Click the desired folder in the **Move Message to Folder** dialog box.
(This folder then appears in the **Move Message into** box.) Here I am moving a message to my Home Business folder:

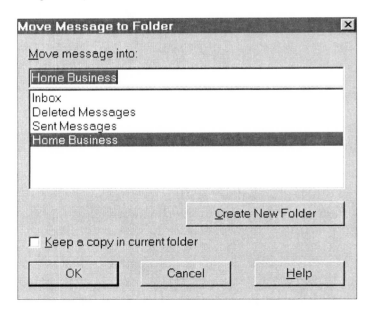

Clicking on *OK* will move the message to the selected folder.

If you want to move the message and keep a copy in the folder from which you are moving it, click the check box by **Keep a copy in current folder.**

Click **OK**

To Read a Message in a Folder

Click the **Read** tab.

Click the arrow in the pull-down **Folder** menu above the message list to open the menu.

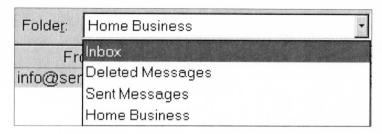

Selecting *Inbox* in the pull-down Folder menu.

Click the appropriate folder.

Open the desired message by clicking on it on the message list.

Saving Messages to a Disk

You may save messages as text files to a floppy disk or to your hard drive with the **Export Message to Text File** command. When you have saved it on a floppy or in the hard drive, you can read it with a word processing program.

Click **File**

Click **Export Message to Text File.** A dialog box will appear.

Click the **Save in** box arrow to locate the folder in which you plan to save the message. (I am saving a message concerning my Juno account in my correspondence file.)

Saving a message as a text file in a folder.

Enter a name for the message in the **File name** box.

Click **Save**

Click **OK**

Working with Attachments

Like many email providers, Juno cautions against opening any attachment that you have not scanned for viruses. We'll get to that momentarily. First...

To Create an Attachment

Before you send any file as an attachment, scan the file with an anti-virus program to be sure that it is not infected. Then...

Click **Write** to start a message.

Click **Attach File** on the left side of the screen.

In the **Attach File** dialog box, locate the folder in which you have the file you wish to attach to the message.

Click the file name, as I did here on Resume:

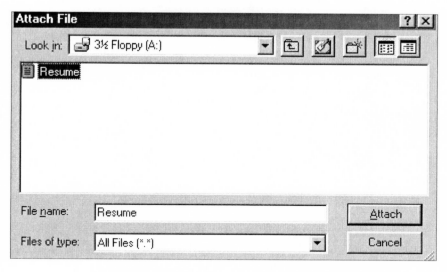

Selecting a file to attach in Juno's *Attach File* dialog box.

Click **Attach.** You will see the attachment noted in the attachment list in the top right corner of the message area.

Proceed with your message as usual.

Saving an Attachment to Disk to Scan for Viruses

Juno indicates that incoming messages have attachments by displaying a paperclip symbol to the left of the sender's name in the message list.

In the **Read** screen message list, click on the message with the attachment.

Click **Show Attachments** in the top-right corner of the message area. Double-click the attachment you wish to scan.

Click **Save File** in the File Attachment dialog box.

Click the **Save in** arrow in the Save Attachment dialog box to choose the folder where you would like to save the attachment.

Click **Save**

Scan the file with your antivirus program. If the attachment is clean, you may then open it if you have the necessary software installed on your computer. Remember that it is not the email program that opens attachments. You open attachments with other programs on your computer, like a word processor, or a spreadsheet, or a media player. If you do not have the relevant program, you will not be able to open the attachment.

To Open an Attachment

In the **Read** screen message list, click the message with the attachment.

Click **Show Attachments**
Double-click the attachment you plan to open.

Click **Open File Now** in the File Attachment dialog box.

Working with the Address Book

The Juno Address book simplifies addressing of your email messages. There you can save the addresses of those who send you messages, and identify each one with a nickname. When you send a message, all you need to enter in the To field is the nickname. "Mom" is a lot easier to type than *janischultz2@provider.com.*

Adding Someone to Your Address Book

Click **Address Book** on the left-hand menu. You'll see this page:

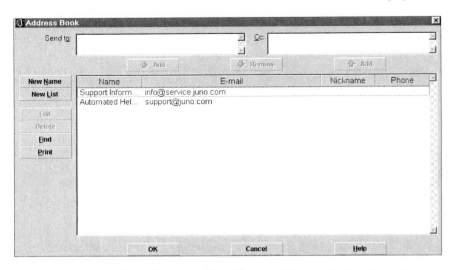

The Address Book may be opened in either the *Write* or the *Read* function.

Click **New Name**. You will see the following box:

Here's where you enter a new name in the Address Book

(If you click Hide Contact Information, the lower part of the box will not display.)

Enter the information in the box. You'll need, at a minimum, the email address and nickname.

Click **OK** when you have entered all the information you wish.

Click **OK** at the bottom of the Address Book to close the book.

Addressing a Message with an Address Book Nickname

Nothing could be easier. With the **Write** screen open, type in the **Send To** field (or the **Cc** field) the nickname you established in the Address Book. Separate multiple nicknames with commas.

Addressing a Message from the Address Book without Using a Nickname

Click **Address Book**

Double-click on a name in the Address Book.

Click **OK** at the bottom of the screen.

Or: click **Address Book**

Click on the pertinent entry or mailing list name.

Click **Add** under the **Send to** box at the top of the screen. This action will lead to the entry of the selected email address in the Send To field on the Write screen.

If you wish to enter an address in the **Cc** field, click **Add** under the Cc box. (If you change your mind about entering an address, click on the entry in the Send To or Cc box; click **Remove**.)

Here in my address book I added Grandma and Dad to the Send To box:

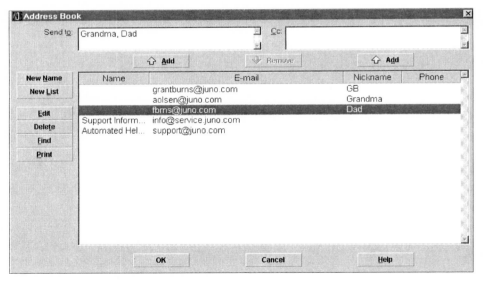

Selecting nicknames from the Address Book.

Click **OK**

You will see the Write screen, with the selected addresses in place.

To Save the Current Message Sender's Address in Your Address Book

Click the message in the Read screen message list whose sender's address you want to save.

Click **Options** (fourth item from left in the top-of-screen toolbar).

Click **Save Current Sender's Address**

Click **OK**

(You *can* have every sender's address automatically added to your Address Book. Juno Help explains how.)

To Create an Address Book Mailing List

A mailing list is a handy tool that enables you to send messages to multiple recipients by entering a single name in the Send To field.

Click **Address Book** in the menu on the left.

Click **New List** in the left-hand menu. You will see the **New Mailing List** dialog box, like this:

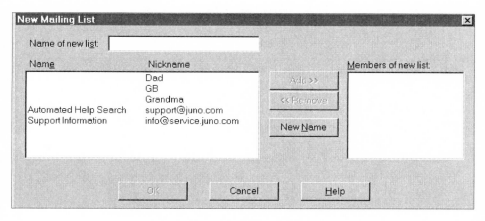

The *New Mailing List* dialog box.

Type the name of the list in the **Name of new list** box. Mailing list names must be unique, and cannot include commas, semi-colons, or parentheses. They are case insensitive. It doesn't matter whether you enter capital letters, lower case, or a mix of the two.

Click each entry in the **Name** list that you want to add to your mailing list. (Names that you add to the mailing list must come from the Name list; to add a new name to the list, click **New Name**.)

Click **Add** for each name you click in the Name list. Juno adds the selected names to the **Members of new list** list.

Click **OK** when you have added all the names you want to your mailing list.

Addressing a Message Using the Mailing List

The easiest way to do this is to type the name of the list in the **Send To** or **Cc** field in the Write screen.

You may also open the Address Book; click on the mailing list; click Add; and click OK. If you remember the names of your mailing lists, as you probably will, it is much easier to type the list name in the Write screen without opening the Address Book.

Other Juno Features

Juno offers a very good Help function, with access by a table of contents, a detailed index, and a search option. The instructions in the Help section are clear, concise, and easy to follow. It's hard to claim that a Help system alone is worth the price of admission—especially when the price is free—but Juno's Help function comes very close to meeting that claim. The Help includes a nice Troubleshooting component, with lots of valuable problem-solving tips.

Juno also offers a substantial range of options for type font, size, and style (bold, italic, etc.); underlining; print and background colors; bullets; text alignment, and other features. Considering that this fine email program comes with Web access, at no charge, it is a top choice for users who want Internet service but who must watch their budgets closely. For those who can afford to shell out just a bit—no more than $10 a month, at this date—for Juno premium service, this is a package that the cost-conscious Internet-savvy user may find hard to resist.

NETSCAPE MESSENGER

Netscape Messenger is another full-service standalone system. It comes free with the popular Netscape Communicator browser. You can obtain Netscape Communicator by going to the company's download site, *http://home.netscape.com/download/*. If you would prefer not to sit through a lengthy downloading session, you can order the browser on a CD-ROM for less than $10 through the same site. Having used both methods of installing browsers, I enthusiastically recommend ordering the CD for any-one working through modem access to the Web. Installing from the CD goes lickety-split compared to downloading from the Web, and is an espe-cially good choice for those new to computing—or for those whose patience does not have a long fuse. I use a version of Netscape Communicator 4.7, which is still available from the company; Netscape's newest browser, Netscape 6.2, might be a better "fit" with the Windows XP operating sys-tem, but 4.7 is a reliable trouper.

Whether you download one of these browsers from the Web, or order the CD, you should find the installation reasonably non-challenging. Just follow Netscape's directions, and you should be OK. To configure your system properly, you will need to know your email address, your password, and the type of mail server you have (POP3 or IMAP). If you do not know some or any of these details, call your Internet Service Provider, who will get you squared away with such necessaries. To specify the proper mail server settings at any time when you are running Netscape Messenger, click **Edit** on the toolbar; click **Preferences**; click **Mail Servers** in the **Category** menu.

Starting Netscape Messenger

Connect to the Internet if you wish to obtain your new mail or to send messages.

Once you have installed the Netscape browser, you can start Messen-ger in various ways:

If you have the browser running, click **Communicator** at the top of the screen. In the Communicator menu, click **Messenger**.

Or: Click on the desktop icon for Netscape Messenger (if you see one on your monitor).

Or do it the long way around:

Click **Start** in the lower left corner of the screen

Place the mouse pointer on **Programs**, then on **Netscape Communi-cator**

Click on **Netscape Messenger**

The Netscape Messenger inbox looks like this (Netscape Messenger software ©2002 Netscape Communications Corporation. Screenshots used with permission.):

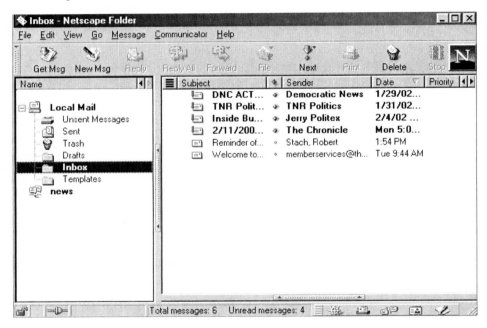

The Inbox. Unopened messages are boldfaced. Used with permission.

Retrieving Messages

To retrieve a message, click on the message summary line in the inbox folder list. The summary line includes the message's subject heading, the sender's name, and the date of sending.

Clicking once on the message line will display the message in the pre-view pane below the message list, like this:

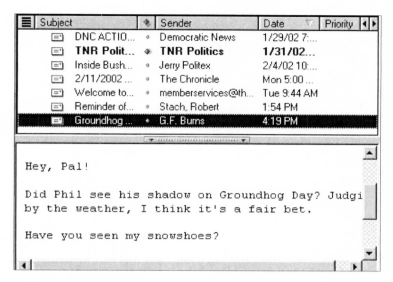

This reduced window shows a message selected, and its content appearing in the preview pane. Used with permission.

(To get rid of the preview pane, click on the bar that separates it from the message list.)

Double-click the message to open it completely.

To Close a Message

Click the X in the top right corner of the screen.

Replying to Messages

With the message that you wish to reply to either open or selected by a single click in the message list, click the **Reply** button on the toolbar. (Click **Reply All** if the message was addressed to multiple recipients, and you want to send your reply to all of them.)

The Netscape Messenger Inbox toolbar. Click Reply to begin a reply to a message. Used with permission.

The Netscape Messenger Composition page will open, like this:

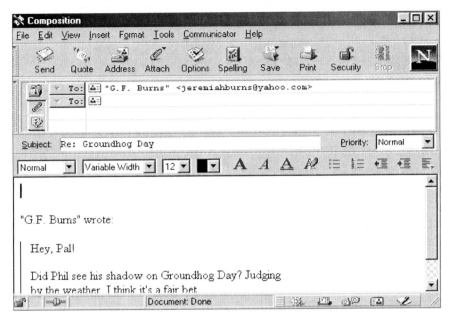

The reply function places the original sender's name in quotation marks before the text of the original message. Used with permission.

The system automatically enters the address of the original sender in the To field, and will include the original subject heading in the Subject field, preceded by Re: ("Regarding").

The cursor appears at the beginning of the Composition page in your reply, above the original message. The helpful note that "Jones, John" (or whoever sent the original message) "wrote" the message is included in the Composition page.

Type your reply to the message, beginning at the point where the cursor automatically appeared. If the original message is brief, feel free to leave the entire message as it is, and send it back with your reply. If the message is long, consider whether it would be helpful to delete portions of it before sending your reply. Leaving some of the original message will assist the recipient, especially if he or she does not read your reply for several days after having sent the original. It will also help you if you save your messages for later review.

To delete portions of the original message, highlight them by holding down the left button on the mouse, and then press the Delete key.

After you complete your reply, click the **Spelling** button on the Composition page toolbar. Netscape Messenger checks your spelling for you, if you direct it to do so. Spell checking this way is a lot easier than fumbling with a conventional dictionary!

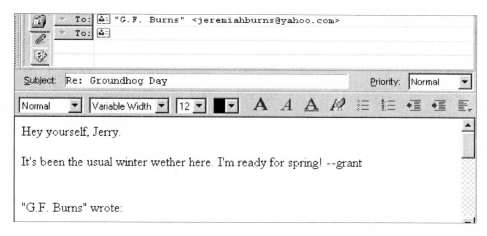

This message needs a little attention to detail! Used with permission.

When you click the Spelling button, the **Check Spelling** box opens:

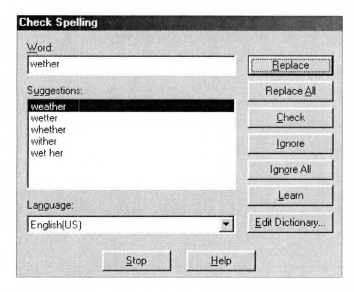

Netscape Messenger is generous with suggestions in its spell checker. Used with permission.

Netscape Messenger found my error in the above message, and is giving me a chance to choose a suggested correction. If the first suggestion suits, click **Replace**. If not, consider other suggestions, click on one, and click Replace.

Or: Put the pointer on the Word field, click once to establish the cursor, and delete the mistaken word. Type in your own correction, and click Replace.

Click **Done** in the Check Spelling box when you have finished this pleasant little chore. Netscape Messenger will return you to the Composition page with your changes in place.

Click **Send** in the upper-left of the toolbar to mail your message.

Composing and Sending a Message

To send a new message, click **New Msg** on the toolbar. The Composition page will open, like this:

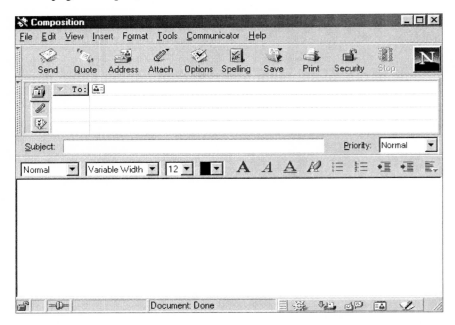

A brand-new Composition page, ready for anything from a love note to a political rant. Used with permission.

Enter a valid email address in the **To** field.

Press the **Tab** key to move the cursor to the *Subject* field.

Type in a word or brief phrase that describes the content of your message.

Press the Tab key again to move the cursor into the message field.

Type your message. Read it to be sure that it says what you mean to say, and then click the Spelling button on the toolbar to vet your orthography. (That's the $14.95 way of saying, "Look for your spelling goofs.") See directions on spell checking under Replying to Messages, above.

All done? Click **Send**. Your message has joined the billions flying through cyberspace. If you want to reread what you sent, click on your Sent folder and open the message in the message list. Unless you specify otherwise in the **Preferences** settings (discussed near the end of this section), Netscape Messenger automatically keeps a copy of sent messages.

Sending to Multiple Recipients

It's easy. Type the addresses into the **To** field; separate them with commas.

Sending Copies

Sometimes it makes more sense to send copies through the **Cc** or **Bcc** function than it does to include everyone whom you want to see the message in the To field. The To field should include your primary recipients; the Cc ("Carbon copy") field should include secondary recipients; the Bcc ("blind carbon copy") field includes recipients whose anonymity you wish to protect from other recipients' awareness. If that sounds a little shady, it might be, although it might also be just what discretion demands. If you wish to read more about the psychosocial business of sending copies, please see my observations in this guide's first part.

To send a copy:

Enter the address(es) of your primary recipient(s) in the To field.

Place the mouse pointer on the first blank line below the primary address(es).

Right click to establish the cursor on the blank line. At the same time, the system will place another To at the left of the line.

Clicking on the new To opens the following menu:

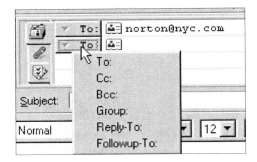

Make choices on copies from this menu. Used with permission.

Click on **Cc**

Type the addresses for the secondary recipient(s).

To send a blind copy, select **Bcc** from the menu.

Saving a Draft

All emailers eventually find it impossible or at least awkward to finish a given message at one sitting. Netscape Messenger makes it easy to save a message in progress so that you can return to it and finish it later, at your convenience. To do it:

Click **File** in the upper-left corner of the Composition page.

Place the mouse pointer on **Save As**

Click **Draft** in the menu that opens from Save As.

Netscape Messenger will place the draft in the **Drafts** folder. To retrieve the draft for later work, click the Drafts folder at the left side of the screen, and double-click on the desired message in the message list.

Forwarding Messages

The matter of forwarding messages raises as many concerns as that of sending copies. Sometimes it's a fine idea; sometimes it's better to be careful. For further thoughts, see my comments on forwarding in this guide's first part.

To forward a message:

Click on the message list on the message you wish to forward, or double-click to open it completely.

Click **Forward** in the toolbar and hold down the mouse button. You will see the following choices for forwarding:

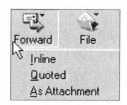

Choices for forwarding. Used with permission.

For a clean look, I prefer the Quoted version, which places the full text of the forwarded message in the Composition page, but which omits the clutter of the original headers. In their place, the system simply precedes the forwarded message with a statement attributing the message to its original sender, for example:

"Smith, John" wrote:

The **inline** option includes the original message headers (subject, date, from and to fields). If you want to be careful to establish a "paper trail" (oops, electron trail), the inline approach would be a good choice.

If you forward **As Attachment**, all you need do is click As Attachment, enter a valid email address in the Composition page that opens, and click Send. Netscape Messenger sends the complete forwarded message as an attachment.

Most of the time, most email users would probably rather receive forwardings in the quoted or inline form, so they don't have to fool around opening attachments.

Deleting Messages

If you have an IMAP mail server:

You may set the deletion preferences.

Click **Edit** on the toolbar.

Click **Preferences** on the Edit menu.

Click **Mail Servers** under **Mail & Newsgroups**

Click **Edit**

Click the **IMAP** tab in the **Mail Server Properties** box.

IMAP server deletion options include moving a deleted message to the Trash folder; using the procedure outline above; and removing the message immediately. In any case, to delete a message, click on the message you want to delete from a message list and click Delete on the toolbar. If you have not set the preferences to remove it immediately, you will either need to remove it by compacting the folder or by emptying the Trash folder.
To compact the folder:

Click on **File** in the upper-left corner of the screen.

Click on **Compact This Folder** in the File menu to purge selected messages.

If you use a POP3 mail server (or if you have your IMAP server send deleted messages to the Trash folder):
Click in the message list on the messages that you want to delete.

Click **Delete**. Marked messages go to the Trash folder. You can recover the messages from the Trash by double-clicking that folder, clicking once on the messages to mark them, and moving them to another folder.

To Clean Out the Trash Folder

Click on **File**

Click **Empty Trash Folder** in the File menu.

Printing Messages

In a message list, double-click the message you wish to print.

Click the **Print** button on the toolbar.

Follow the usual routine with your printer.

Working with Folders

Effective use of folders is vital to good email management. The default folders provided by any email system are adequate only if you send and receive few messages. Folders are, in effect, electronic storage bins where you stash messages united by one or more characteristics. One folder might contain all the messages you have received from your son in college; another might be the place you file the messages from your book club members; another holds the messages from your spouse, and so on.

Creating a Folder

Click **File** in the upper-left corner of the screen

Click **New Folder**

Type the new folder name in the dialog box. Be sure that the folder name has a clear connection to the content that you plan for the folder. "Miscellaneous" is not a good folder name!

Click the arrow to open the subfolder menu and select a place to put the new folder.

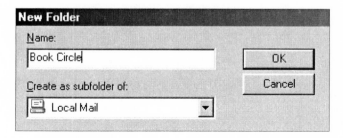

Here I'm making my new folder, **Book Circle**, a subset of my **Local Mail**. Used with permission.

Click **OK**

You will see the new folder established in the place you designated.

To Save a Message in a Folder

One way...

Click on the message in a message list

Hold down the left mouse button and drag the message over the folder where you wish to place it.

Release the mouse button to drop the message into the folder.

(If you are using an IMAP server, the above drag & drop routine places a copy of the message into the chosen folder, and leaves the original in the message list. To remove the message from the list, use the deletion procedure described above.)

Another way...

Right-click on the message in the message list.

In the open menu, place the mouse pointer on **Move Message**

Click on the folder in which you wish to place the message.

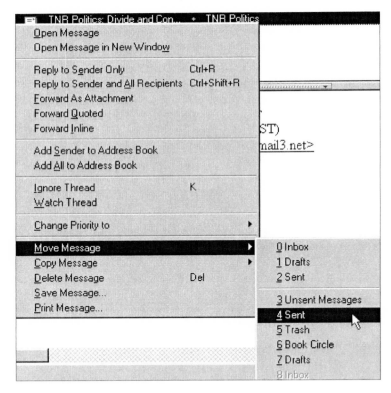

The menu that opens on the right will list available folders. Used with permission.

This method will mark the message in the message list for deletion. Delete by following the instructions noted above.

Yet another way...

Click the **File** button on the toolbar (directly above the message list, *not* the File in the upper-left corner). The folder menu will open.

Another folder list for filing messages. Used with permission.

Click on the file where you want to place the message.

Saving Messages to a Disk

You may save messages to a floppy disk or to a folder in your computer. To do it:

Click the message on the message list to select it if it is not already open.

Click **File** in the upper-left corner.

Place mouse pointer on **Save As**

Click **File**

In the **Save Message As** box, select a place in your computer (or on the floppy disk) where you want to save the message.

Click **Save**

Working with Attachments

An attachment is a computer file that rides piggyback on an email message. It might be a text file, a sound file, a picture, or another type of file that your email recipient can open—provided his or her computer has software that can handle the program in which the file was created. If you send a sound file as an attachment to someone who does not have software able to handle the file, the attachment will be pointless. It is worth remembering that it is not the email program that opens attachments, but other programs on the computer that do the job.

Sending an Attachment

With a message Composition page open, click the **Attach** button (the one with the paper clip) directly above the message header fields.

Netscape Messenger allows you to attach a file, a Web page (by entering the page's URL), or a Personal Address Card (which you can set up through the Preferences options). Let's attach a file:

Click **File** in the Attach menu

In the **Enter File to Attach** box, find and double-click the file you wish to attach. Here I have selected the A: drive from which to attach a file:

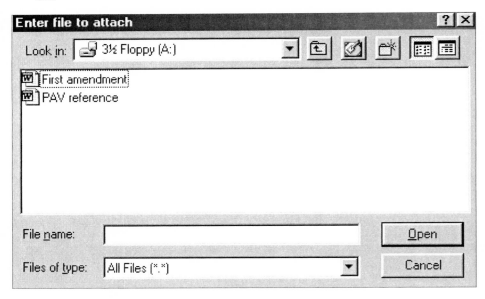

I've selected a place to choose an attachment; now I need to pick which file to attach. Used with permission.

The attached file will appear in the headers area, like this:

Some lucky soul will receive my thoughts on the First Amendment. Used with permission.

Notice that the attachment name appears where you would normally see the address of the recipient. Don't worry: If you entered the address, it hasn't gone away. To see it, click the Address Message button (the top button at the left of the headers field box).

Complete and send your message as usual.

Viewing Attachments

Netscape Messenger offers different ways to handle incoming attachments: You may view image and Web page attachments inline (in the body of the message). With the message open, click on View; click on View Attachments Inline in the view menu.

You may view image and Web page attachments as links. With a message open in which the attachments appear inline, click View; click View Attachments as Links.

You may view attachments as icons: Click the paper clip icon to the right of a message header in the open message. Here in the body of a message that came with an attachment we learn the name of the attachment and the program in which it was created:

First Amendment.doc	**Name:** First Amendment.doc **Type:** WINWORD File (application/msword) **Encoding:** base64

Anyone whose computer has MS Word installed should be able to open this attachment. Used with permission.

Clicking on the link allows either opening the attachment or saving it to a disk.

To Open an Attachment

Do not open any attachment before scanning it for viruses! Save the message with the attachment to a folder in your computer, or on a floppy disk, and scan it with your antivirus software. If it checks out clean, you may proceed. If you have not scanned the attachment, do not even think about opening it. You could set loose a hungry virus in your computer that will do expensive damage.

The fact that the attachment comes from a trusted correspondent is not sufficient reason to open it without virus scanning. Email users often send viruses in attachments without intending to do so.

Click the link for the attachment in the message, or double-click the attachment icon. Netscape Messenger will ask you if you want to open the attachment or save it to a disk. If you have scanned the message for viruses and it appears clean, go ahead and open it. If you have not scanned it, save it and scan it.

I know: I keep telling you to "save it and scan it." If you ever find your computer hog-tied by a virus, you will understand my harping on this theme! By the way, if you want to be a considerate emailer, you will also not *send* any attachments before checking them to be sure they don't carry viruses. Doing otherwise is like coughing in public without covering your mouth. Maybe worse!

Working with the Address Book

The Netscape Messenger Address Book is a useful tool to expedite addressing messages to both individuals and groups. To use it, you need to establish entries in it.

You may add the sender of a message to your address book while you're in an open message:

Click **Message** at the top of the toolbar.

Click **Add Sender to Address Book** in the Message menu (as shown at top of page 163):

This action opens a **New Card** window in which you may enter a nickname for your contact, and other information, as shown on page 163:

After completing the New Card, click **OK** to add the new contact to your address book.

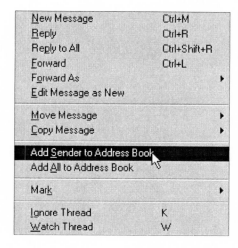

The Message Menu. Used with permission.

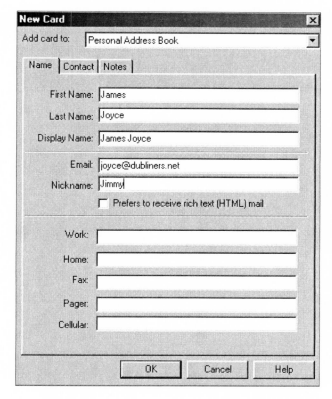

Filling out a New Card for a contact. Used with permission.

You may also work on your address book without being in an open message:

Click **Communicator** at the top of the screen

Click **Address Book** in the menu

Click **New Card** to create an individual entry

Creating a Mailing List

Click **Communicator**

Click **Address Book**

Click **New List**. You will see the **Mailing List** box, in which you can add entries to your list (or, if you have an established mailing list, make changes). I have populated this mailing list with entries for my imaginary book circle:

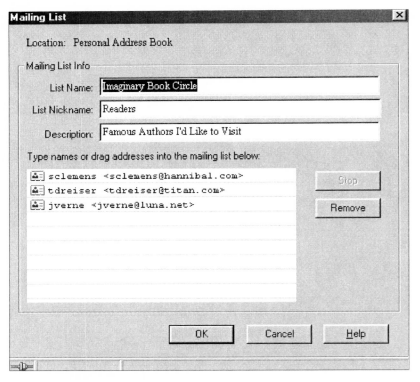

If I address this message to Readers, it will go to the people included in this mailing list. Used with permission.

Addressing Messages with the Address Book

Click the **Address** button in the open Composition page.

Double-click the people or groups to which you want to send your message.

Click **OK**

Finish your message as usual.

You may also type the nicknames in the To field of people or groups in your address book. Netscape Messenger replaces the nicknames with proper addresses when you press the Tab key to move the cursor down to the Subject field.

Working Offline

You may compose new messages for later sending or open and manage messages in folders in your Local folders without being online.

Composing a Message Offline for Later Mailing

With Netscape Messenger running, click **New Message** and compose your message as usual.

When done, click **File** in the Composition page. Click **Send Later** in the File menu. The system will save the message in your Unsent Messages folder. When you connect to the Internet, you can send messages in the Unsent file:

Click **File**

Click **Send Unsent Messages**

You can synchronize your Netscape Messenger mail for an optimum relationship between online and offline work. This topic is beyond the scope of a beginning guide, but you can find the directions in the system Help function by looking in the index for **offline**.

Preferences

Netscape Messenger allows considerable flexibility in how you handle your mail through its Preferences options. To see and set (or reset) your preferences:

Click **Edit**

Click **Preferences**
You will see the following box:

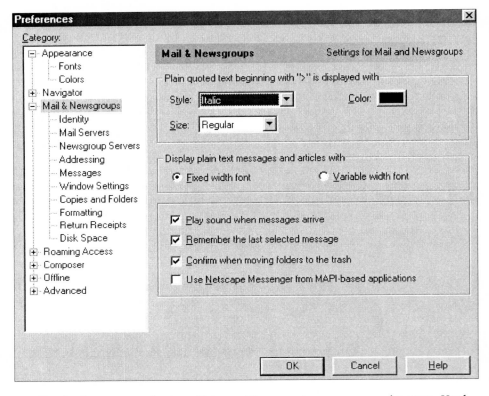

Here's where you can fine tune Netscape Messenger to your own requirements. Used with permission.

Click on any of the entries under **Mail & Newsgroups** to make adjustments.

Filtering

Netscape Messenger's message filtering system allows you to fine-tune the program so that it automatically files incoming messages into the appropriate folders (including Trash), depending on criteria you select. These criteria include sender, subject, date, and so on. For directions, look for **email filters** in the **Help** index.

Speaking of Help...

The program's useful Help function allows access by both table of contents and index.

In sum, Netscape Messenger is a full-featured program that is especially handy for those who rely on Netscape Communicator as their primary Web browser. It is easy to learn and operate, and Netscape's prominence in the marketplace suggests that its Messenger system will be with us—probably with continuing upgrades—for the reasonably long haul.

OUTLOOK EXPRESS

No free email program is perfect (what is?), but I like Microsoft's Outlook Express. The major concern with the program that I have been able to identify is its susceptibility to viruses, but there are ways around that, and this section will include some tips in that regard. I like OE because it is both easy to use and very flexible. It takes a bit more time to master than most Web-based programs, simply because of its many features, but the most basic functions are quick learners.

One of the most appealing traits of Outlook Express is that you can set it up to work in synchronization with Microsoft's Web email, Hotmail (described in its own section here), thus allowing a reasonably seamless interplay between the Outlook Express system installed on your computer, and the Hotmail you may use at the library across town, or across the country.

Outlook Express is a flexible free email program, with a large array of options. Many of them amount to more than the majority of casual emailers will likely need to use or understand. I am focusing here, as elsewhere, on the basics; one could easily write a book-length manual concerning Outlook Express by itself. Fortunately, Outlook Express offers an excellent Help function, with a highly-detailed index. It is easy to click Help, go to the index, and from there find and view information on a wealth of system topics.

Creating a New Account

Outlook Express comes in the package with the Web browser, Internet Explorer, known in shorthand as "IE." Outlook Express runs on IE. Chances are very good that if you have a computer, it came with IE already installed on it, and Outlook Express waiting to be set up. If you do not have IE, you can obtain it, and the other components in its package, without charge from Microsoft's IE download site:

http://www.microsoft.com/windows/ie/downloads

Follow Microsoft's directions for download and installation, and you should be OK. The directions are straightforward. Before downloading, of course, you will need to have an account with an Internet Service Provider (ISP) so that you can dial into the Internet and the World Wide Web. (See notes on ISPs in this guide's introduction.) When you set up Outlook Express, you will need an email address and system password, and the names of your incoming—POP3 (Post Office Protocol), IMAP, or HTTP protocols—and your outgoing SMTP (Simple Mail Transfer Protocol) mail server. Don't know? Don't worry. Call your ISP and ask.

Unlike the Web email programs described in this guide, Outlook Express is a program on your computer. You do not need to login to use it, but you do need to run the program to use it. You can work in Outlook Express without being connected to the Internet, but you do, of course, need to be connected to the Internet to send and receive messages. You may, however, download your new mail to your computer, disconnect, and read the new messages offline, and even compose replies that you can send when you reconnect. If you have one telephone line and a teenager in the house, this is a plus for family good feeling.

To Check and Read Mail in the Outlook Express Inbox

You do not need to be connected to the Internet to read mail in Outlook Express, but you do need to connect to it to download any new mail that is waiting for you in your system's server.

Connect to the Internet

Start your Outlook Express program. If you placed a shortcut on the computer desktop, you can double-click on the shortcut to start Outlook

Express. You may also start the program from the Start menu: Click the Start button in the bottom left of your screen; put the mouse pointer on Programs; click on Outlook Express in the Programs menu.

You'll see the following page (with your name in place of mine!—and not necessarily the Hotmail entry in the Folders column; I set up Outlook Express to work with my Hotmail account. You may set up yours to work with your ISP account.)

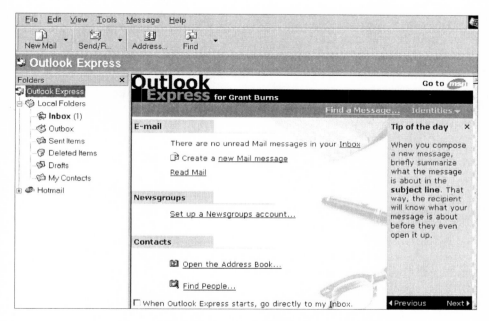

The Outlook Express opening screen.

Your system server downloads any new mail for you into your Inbox folder. You may at this point disconnect from the Internet.

Notice the checkbox at the bottom of the screen. If you want to bypass this opening screen, click this box and you will begin Outlook Express at your Inbox. At this opening screen, however, you do receive an immediate alert to the existence of new mail: Under the "Email" heading, the system tells you how many unread messages your Inbox contains.

From the opening page, click on Inbox, Read Mail, or Unread Mail (the presence of the second two categories depending on whether there is new mail in your Inbox). The system will take you to the Inbox, and will display a list of any messages there, noting sender, subject, and date and time received, like this:

!	0	▽	From	Subject	Received ∧	
			Microsoft Outlook Ex...	Welcome to Outlook Express 5	12/4/01 8:51 PM	
			Security Bulletin Add...	SUBSCRIBE MICROSOFT_SECURITY	12/5/01 9:55 PM	
			Security Bulletin Add...	Welcome to the Microsoft Product Security ...	12/7/01 2:53 PM	
			Microsoft	**Microsoft Security Notification Bullet...**	**12/20/01 1:...**	
			Microsoft	Microsoft Security Bulletin MS01-060	12/20/01 10:27...	

An inbox message list.

Click the message line twice to see the message open in a window that you can expand to the full screen. OR: Click the message once to see the message in the Preview Pane below the list of messages. Click the "X" button in the upper-right corner of the browser to close the full-screen window, or click **File** and **Close** on the pull-down menu at the upper left. You can also press the **Alt** and **F4** keys together to close the message. An open message looks like this:

From:	Microsoft
Date:	Thursday, December 20, 2001 1:35 PM
To:	captstormfield@hotmail.com
Subject:	Microsoft Security Notification Bulletin MS01-059

-----BEGIN PGP SIGNED MESSAGE-----

- --
Title: Unchecked Buffer in Universal Plug and Play can Lead
      to System Compromise
Date: 20 December 2001
Software: Windows 98, Windows 98SE, Windows ME, Windows XP
Impact: Run code of attacker's choice
Max Risk: Critical
Bulletin: MS01-059

Microsoft encourages customers to review the Security Bulletin at:
http://www.microsoft.com/technet/security/bulletin/MS01-059.asp.

An open message in the inbox.

As you see, Microsoft has found a vulnerable spot in the system, and is advising users to check a security bulletin. We'll have more on that imminently.

VIRUS ALERT: Certain viruses might be able to pass into your computer from the Outlook Express Preview Pane. Reportedly, it is not necessary to double-click the message to open it fully to allow such viruses to obtain a foothold in your machine. There are at least two ways around this threat: Disable the Preview Pane, or obtain from Microsoft a download of Internet Explorer that contains a "fix" for the hole in the pane. You might try the first option for the short term, but it would be wise to make a proper "patch" on your browser by going to the Microsoft site (noted above).

Disabling the Preview Pane

Click **View** at the top of the Outlook Express screen.

Click **Layout**

In the **Preview Pane** portion of the Layout box, see that the checkbox next to "Show preview pane" is not checked. If it is checked, click the box to remove the check.

Click **Apply**, and then click **OK**.

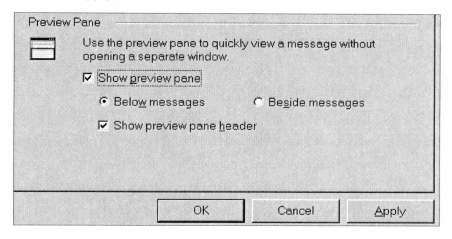

Click the check box next to *Show preview pane* to close the pane.

Outlook Express uses Internet Explorer to view messages and process certain attachments. I had an older version of IE 5.01 on my computer that lacked "Service Pack 2," which prevents that version of IE from automatically running programs embedded in previewed messages. I downloaded from the Microsoft site noted above a newer version with Service Pack 2.

My objective here is not to teach downloading; there are better places to go to find out how to do that (although it often is very easy). Be aware, though, that computer software, including Web browsers, is in a state of continuing evolution and discovery—as are viruses! If you are using a very old version of a browser, you will almost surely want to update it to take advantage of new features and improved security. Check back with your browser's source for updates, problem patches, and other information to keep your computer running smoothly. It won't hurt to dip into some of the plentiful literature online concerning computer functionality.

Regardless of what email system you use, you need to take reasonable steps to protect your data and your computer from what Microsoft generally refers to as "malicious users" or "malicious operators." The adjective is well chosen, for that is what they are. If you use Internet Explorer, you should check Microsoft's Web site on a reasonably regular basis to see if it notes any new patches to download that will enhance the security of the versions of IE or Outlook Express on your computer. These downloads are easy to accomplish, usually do not take very long, and the installation is simple. To bring up a tedious term that I have used elsewhere in this guide, you do not need to be "computer literate" to take care of this basic computer housekeeping. If you can read and follow straightforward directions and type a little bit, you can do the job as well as a veteran computer programmer.

The Internet Explorer Critical Updates Site

At this date, the URL (Uniform Resource Locator, or "Web address") for Microsoft's "Critical Updates" page for Internet Explorer is:

http://www.microsoft.com/windows/ie/downloads/critical/default.asp

This page contains announcements of system updates that Microsoft provides "to help resolve known issues and protect your computer from known security vulnerabilities." Each update features a free download that Microsoft has developed to address the problems described. When you check the updates, you'll need to know the version of IE that you use. (Different versions require different updates.) To find out, open the browser's pull-down **Help** menu, and click **About Internet Explorer**. The version of IE on your machine will appear in the ensuing window.

I cannot urge you strongly enough to check and follow through on the IE "Critical Updates" before using Outlook Express! Some of these updates directly concern the email system. The wise emailer would no sooner habitually use Outlook Express without downloading recommended system patches than he or she would deliberately prop the back door wide open before going off on a long vacation. The vacationer doing that could come home to find rats in the house; the emailer who ignores security safeguards could well find electronic rodents in the family computer. Microsoft has taken the time to develop these updates for your security; take your own time (it won't be very long) to take advantage of them. Another Microsoft site especially useful for Outlook Express users contains the latest information on the program:

http://www.microsoft.com/windows/oe/

Yet another site worth bookmarking is Woody Leonhard's Windows newsletter, *Woody's Watch* (*http://www.woodyswatch.com/*). There you'll find many easily-understood tips on how to have a happier computing experience. The chief point to grasp: The computing environment is always changing. You need to put a little effort into following the changes so that you can enjoy yourself online, rather than become pestered by needless problems. There are many adept people at Microsoft and elsewhere doing the main work of tracking developments and technical glitches and fixes. Pay them some attention. You'll be glad you did.

Composing a Message

Remember that you do not need to be connected to the Internet to compose mail in Outlook Express. You can be connected if you like, but it isn't necessary. Unlike the Web-based email programs, which are out there on the Web, this one is right on your computer.

Start the Outlook Express program.

Click **New Mail** on the main toolbar in the top left corner of the screen. Your **New Message** window will appear.

Enter a valid email address in the **To** field and press the Tab key to move the cursor to the **Subject** field. Type in a subject that reasonably characterizes your message. Press the Tab key again. This should move the cursor into the message field.

Write your message. Are you a good speller? No matter: You'll still want to take time to check the spelling in your message. Click on **ABC Spelling** on the message toolbar. Here's a short message I composed for my email alter ego, Captain Stormfield. Notice anything odd about it?

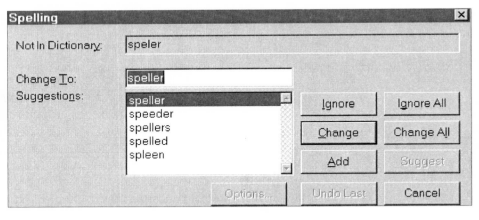

To: captstormfield@hotmail.com

Cc:

Subject: How's My Spelling Today?

Hi, Captain.

You know, I have never been a very good speler. I'm glad Outlook Express can help!

--Grant

A message with a problem.

Outlook Express will look through your message for misspellings. If it finds any, or thinks it finds any, it will probably give you alternate choices for the word or words that troubled it. You may pick one of the choices and click **Change** to change the spelling in the message. You may prefer your own spelling (sometimes spell checkers get a little fussy, and even a little stupid, about what words are "right." Don't let the spell checker bully you). To accept the system's suggested correction of my spelling error, I'll click **Change** in the **Spelling** box.

Spelling

Not In Dictionary: speler

Change To: speller

Suggestions:
speller
speeder
spellers
spelled
spleen

Ignore   Ignore All
Change   Change All
Add   Suggest
Options...   Undo Last   Cancel

Outlook Express knows how to spell "speller"! Click *Change* to make the correction.

When you're through spell checking, the system will show you a box containing the statement, "The spelling check is complete." Click **OK** in the box. Click **Send** to send the message with any corrected spellings to your Outbox folder. If you're already online, clicking Send at this point will send the message to its recipients. If you're not online, you will need to connect.

If you're offline, Outlook Express will put the message in your Outbox when you click Send.

When you have connected with the Internet, click the **Send/Receive All** button on the toolbar. Your message will be off into cyberspace.

Sending Messages in Plain Text

Outlook Express is capable of sending messages dressed up in considerable finery, with HTML formatting backed by a wide variety of stationery that provides decorative setting for your emails. Some of your recipients' mail programs may not be able handle all the goodies that Outlook Express gives you to, well, *express* yourself. To maximize the likelihood that no one has a problem with your message format, you can send messages in unadorned fashion in Plain Text. To do it, with your New Message window open:

Click **Format** on the message toolbar.

Click **Plain Text** in the Format menu.

You can, if you wish, make Plain Text your default format for new messages, replies, and forwarding:

Click **Tools** on the main toolbar.

Click **Options**

Click the **Send** tab.

Under **Mail Sending Format**, click **Plain Text**.

Even with the default set to Plain Text, you can revert in an individual message to HTML format by clicking Format and then clicking Rich Text (HTML).

Saving a Copy of Your Sent Message

Outlook Express's default setting results in a copy of each message you send going into your Sent Items folder. This feature is helpful; you will occasionally want to retrieve messages that you have sent to remind yourself of one point or another that you made. Unlike the free Web-based email systems, Outlook Express will save copies on your hard drive, so that you do not need to be preoccupied with the amount of space that they consume. (If you work with Outlook Express and Hotmail in tandem, the system will save copies in the Hotmail Web system. You can easily move the copies from Hotmail to your hard drive by clicking and dragging a message from one to the other.)

Although it is often helpful to retain copies of the messages that you send, you will want to review these messages on a reasonably regular basis so that your "Sent" folder does not become overburdened with messages. On review, you will probably decide to delete many sent messages; others you will probably move to various other folders that you have set up for effective organization. (See "Working with Folders," below.)

Sending to Multiple Recipients

Enter addresses as usual in the **To** (or Cc or Bcc) field. Separate the addresses with semicolons.

Sending Copies

Use the **Cc** ("carbon copy") field if you want to send a copy of a message to someone other than its primary recipient. The **Bcc** ("blind carbon copy") field is normally not shown in the **New Message** window. To include it, click **View** and **All Headers** on the message toolbar. As I have mentioned elsewhere in this guide, be careful how you use the Bcc feature. It's called "blind" because the primary recipient of the message will not be aware that you have sent a copy of it to anyone other than those who may be listed in the Cc field. There are times when a blind copy makes good sense, both from perspectives of discretion and compassion. Using the blind copy could save the primary recipient, or the addressee in the blind copy field pointless embarrassment, or avoid further complicating what might already be an awkward situation. Used excessively and carelessly, blind copies can give the recipients of your emails the impression that you are not a person of candor.

Saving a Draft

For many reasons, you may sometimes want to save a message in progress. You may need time to think about it; you might need to walk the dog; you may have been staring into the computer monitor all day and have developed a dandy headache. In any case, there is no need to throw away your half-completed message. To save a draft at any point in the message:

Click **File** on the message toolbar to open the pull-down File menu.

Click **Save**

The system will save the message in your Drafts folder.

It's easy to retrieve a draft message for further work.

To close the message you saved as a draft, click the X in the upper-right corner of the screen.

To retrieve the draft, click the **Drafts** folder on the left side of the screen. The message will appear on the folder list. Click on the message line, and it will open for you to finish. If you want, you can save it again.

Saving Messages to a Floppy Disk or Elsewhere on Your Computer

When you save a message in one of your folders, you are saving it on your hard drive. You may, if you wish, save it elsewhere than in your Outlook Express program. To do so:

Click the message to open it.

Click **File** in the upper-left corner of the message toolbar.

Click **Save As** in the file menu.

Designate a file on your hard drive or on a floppy disk where you want to save the message. You can save the message in mail (.eml), text (.txt) or HTML (.htm) format.

Click **Save** (as I would do here if I wanted to save my message on spelling to my floppy disk):

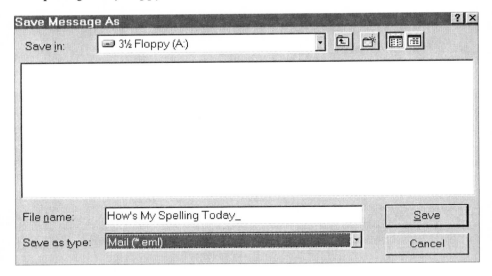

Clicking on *Save* will save this file to a floppy disk.

Replying to a Message

With the message open either in the Preview Pane or the full window, click **Reply** on the **message** toolbar. Check the **To** field in the reply to make sure that your message is going to the intended recipient. Type your message (usually above the original, to facilitate easy chronological tracking if this develops into a long exchange).

Unless the original message is very long, it's better to include it, particularly if you're answering questions that it contains. The sender may not see your reply for some time (some people do manage not to check their email several times a day!), and may find your reply baffling without the helpful reminder of the original message. If, however, you want to edit out all or part of the original, highlight the unneeded bits and press your delete key.

Click **Send** in the upper left corner, and your message is off.

Outlook Express includes a **Reply All** button in the Reply mode. Use this feature when you want everyone addressed in the original To field to see your response. Be careful not to click **Reply All** unless you really do want everyone to see what you have to say!

Forwarding Messages

With a message open, click **Forward** in the message toolbar. Enter the email address of your intended recipient, include a message above the original (your addition may be as brief as "fyi"), and click **Send**.

Deleting Messages

It's easy in Outlook Express. With the message open, either in the full screen or the Preview Pane, click **Delete** on the message toolbar. The system will discard the unwanted message. You may also delete a message without opening it (handy for obvious junk mail): select the message in the message list; click **Delete** on the toolbar.

Change your mind about that deletion? You can retrieve a deleted message by opening the Deleted Items folder, and dragging the message back to drop into the Inbox or another folder.

You can empty all deleted items by selecting the Deleted Items folder. Click the **Edit** menu on the main toolbar. Click **Empty Deleted Items Folder**, as I would here if I wanted to clean out my Deleted Items folder:

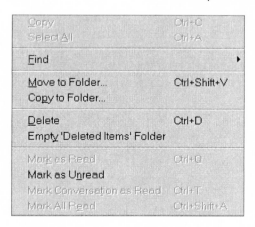

Click on *Empty 'Deleted Items' Folder* to discard unwanted messages.

Blocking Messages

Outlook Express does not support filtering junk mail so that it goes directly to your Deleted Items, but it does allow you to block systematically messages from a specific sender or domain. (The domain is the name after the "@" symbol in an email address). Blocking either a sender or domain results in any messages from that source going straight into your Deleted Items folder, and will help minimize spam and other junk email in your Inbox . To do it:

At your Inbox, select a message from a source you would like to block.

Click **Message** on the toolbar.

On the **Message** menu, click **Block Sender:**

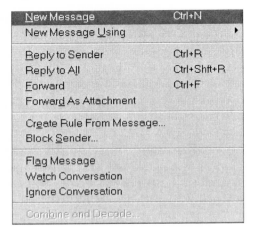

Message menu with *Block Sender* command.

Printing Messages

Open your message and click the **Print** icon in the message toolbar. Make the choices you prefer to tell your printer what to do.

Working with Folders

Folders are the places where you store your messages. Outlook Express offers five default folders: **Inbox, Outbox, Sent Items, Deleted Items**, and **Drafts**. Even if you start your email experience on a small scale, with a message here and there, you will almost surely want to add further folders. The more email you send, the more you receive, and vice versa. It probably won't be long before those default folders just don't do the job you need regarding organization of your messages.

Creating a Folder

If you would like to add a folder to your Outlook Express:

Click the pull-down **File** menu in the upper left of your screen in the main toolbar.

Place the mouse pointer on **Folder**.

Click **New** in the menu that appears when you point to Folder.

Type a name for the folder in the **Folder name** box. Reflect for a moment on what will make a good name. Ideally, the name will be one that immediately associates in your memory with the content of the folder. Carelessly-named folders can be real headaches: What hope do you have of remembering the messages you stored in a folder named "Random Stuff"?

Choose the location for the folder. If I click on **OK** here, after selecting Local Folders, my new Home Business folder will join my Local Folders list.

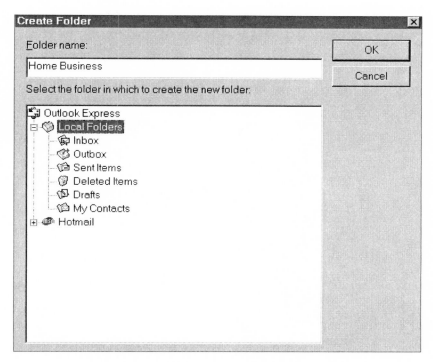

Creating a new folder.

Click **OK**

Outlook Express will show your new folder in the Folders list at the left side of the screen.

Saving Messages to a Folder

There are two ways, one quick, the other quicker. The quicker way:

Do the "drag and drop" routine:

Click on the message line in the message list to highlight it.

Place the mouse pointer on the message, hold down the left button of your mouse, and keep it down while you drag the pointer over to the folder list.

When you have the pointer on top of the folder where you want to store your message, release the button. The message will go into that folder.

The quick way:

With the message open, click **File** on the message toolbar to open the File menu.

Click either **Move to folder** or **Copy to folder**. Outlook Express will open a window that shows your folders; click the folder where you want to save the message. Note that if you select **Move to folder**, the message will exist only in that folder. If you select **Copy to folder**, it will remain where it is as well as going into the selected folder. For example, if you are working on a message in your Drafts folder and, using Move to folder, you place it in your Home Business folder, it will no longer be in your Drafts folder.

Click on *Move to Folder* to open the list of folders available to you.

To Delete a Folder

Click the folder in the **Folders** list.

Click the **File** menu.

Place the pointer on **Folder**.

Click **Delete**

Outlook Express will not allow deletion of the default folders: Inbox, Outbox, Sent Items, Deleted Items, or Drafts.

Working with Attachments

An attachment is a previously existing file that you include with an email. It could be a picture found on the Internet, a document from your word processing program, a spreadsheet, even a song or a movie clip.

Do not attach a file, or open an attachment, unless you have scanned it for viruses and are confident that it is clean. Microsoft Windows does not include an antivirus function. The company recommends that users run an antivirus program on any attachment to be sure that it is safe.

To Attach a File to a Message

With a new message open, click **Insert** on the message toolbar. (If you wish to insert a picture, a link to a Web site (a "hyperlink"), or text from a file, click anywhere in the message field before clicking Insert.

Click **File Attachment** on the Insert menu.

Locate the file you want to attach in your computer.

Click on the file to select it. Here I've selected "GM '55" on a floppy disk in my A: drive (as shown on top page 184):

Click the **Attach** button.

You will see the file indicated in the message header's Attach box, as shown on page 184.

Click **Send** to send the message and its attachment.

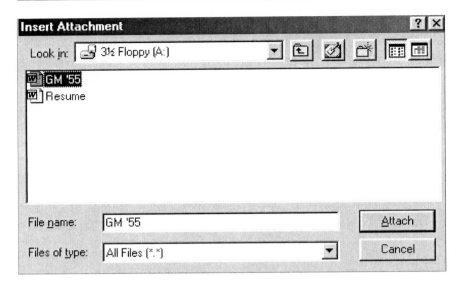

I have chosen a file on a floppy disk to attach to a message.

The attachment is noted in the *Attach* field.

To View an Attachment

Unless you are confident that the attachment does not contain a virus, do not open it for viewing in Outlook Express. Instead, save it to a folder on your computer or on a floppy disk, and scan it for viruses before opening it. To save it:

With the message open:

Click the **File** menu on the message toolbar.

Click **Save Attachments**

Select a folder or disk to which you want to save the attachment. (It's helpful to use the "Browse" feature.)

Click **Save**. (I'm saving this attachment to the My Documents file, since it's a Microsoft Word document):

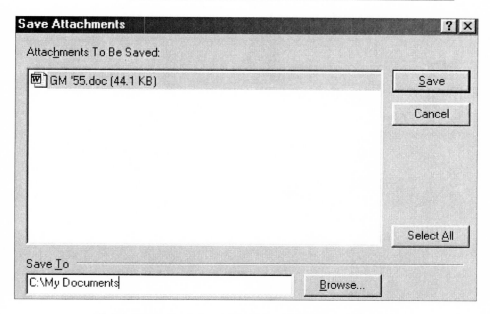

Click *Save* to save the attachment to a folder for scanning.

After scanning the attachment for viruses, to view it:

Click the paper clip icon in the upper right corner if you are in the preview pane.

Double-click the file attachment line that opens below the paper clip.

Alternatively, you may:

Open the message and double-click the file attachment line in the message header at the top of the open message window. The attachment will open, if your computer has the software required for the file. Remember that the email program is not responsible for opening attachments: You open attachments with other software on your computer.

Working with the Address Book

The Address Book gives you a handy place to file information about people, groups, and organizations. Its uses are many, but we'll concentrate here on its primary purpose: to enhance the convenience of your emailing. You can insert names from the Address Book directly into your message **To** field; you can also create groups to which you can send messages with a greatly simplified addressing procedure. Before you can do any of this, you need to put some names and email addresses into your Address Book!

Adding a Contact to Your Address Book

Open the Address Book by clicking on the book icon on the main toolbar (2d item from the right).

Select the folder on the left side of the screen where you want to add a contact. I'll add a contact in Main Identity's Contacts. (Each person who uses Outlook Express on a given computer can have his or her own identity, enabling independent management of emails. The Outlook Express Help function explains this advanced feature. If only one person uses your email, you'll most likely have only the Main Identity.)

Preparing to add a contact.

Click **New** on the toolbar to open the pull-down menu.

Click **New Contact** to open the **Properties** box.

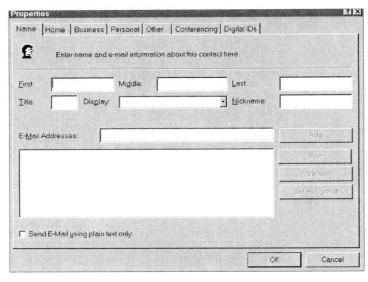

The Address Book contact Properties box.

Type at least the first and last names on the **Name** tab.

Add any information you wish on the other tabs. Be sure to enter an email address for your contact!

Click **Add**

Click **OK** on any of the tabbed screens to complete adding the contact.

To Send a Message Using the Address Book

Click **New Mail** on the toolbar.

To put addresses from the Address Book into the To field, click the icon resembling a book in the New Message window next to the **To** field (or the **Cc** or **Bcc** fields), and select names. (For the Bcc field, click **View**, and select **All Headers**.)

For each name you select, click **To** (or **Cc** or **Bcc**) in the **Select Recipients** window.

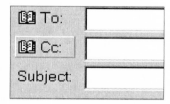

Notice the Address Book icons next to the *To* and *Cc* fields.

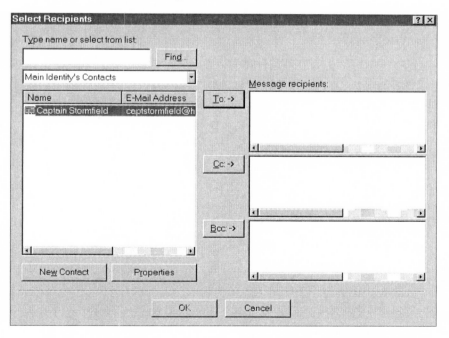

To address a message to Captain Stormfield, we'll select his name at the left and click the *To* button.

When you have selected all the names you want, click **OK**. The selected contacts will be addressed in your New Message headers.

Complete the message as usual.

Alternatively (and more likely, if you're sending a message to someone you know well whose name is in the Address Book):

Simply type the name of your intended recipient in the **To** field. Assuming the name you type there is the same as the name you entered for that person in the address book, Outlook Express will address the message correctly.

To Create a Group in the Address Book

If you regularly send messages to a group of people—your book club, bowling team, church volunteers—it is much easier to enter member addresses through the address book than to bang them into the To field one by one. With a mailing group established, to send a message to everyone in the group all you need to do is to type the group name into the To field.

Open the Address Book.

Select the folder where you want to put the group.

Click **New** on the toolbar.

Click **New Group**

You'll see the **Properties** dialog box open, as shown on top of page 189.

Pick a name for the group and type it into the **Group Name** box.

Add People to the Group

In the open group Properties box:

Click **Select Members** on the right side of the box.

Click any name from the Address Book list to add to the group.

Click **Select**

Click **OK**. Below I add Captain Stormfield to a group (as seen at bottom of page 189):

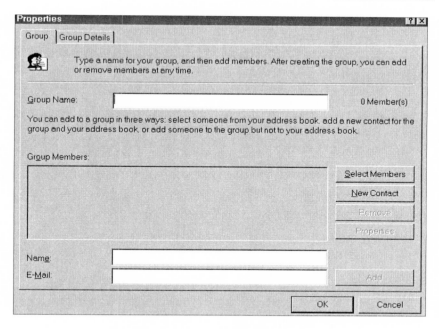

The Properties box for groups.

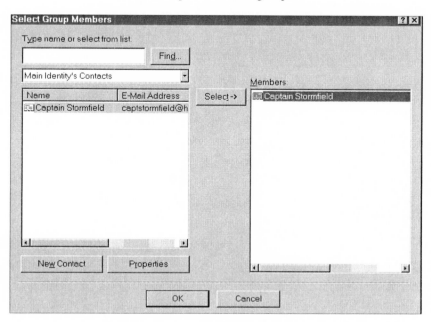

Selecting a name to include in a group.

Or, type the name and email address of the person you want to add to the group in the **Properties** dialog box

Click **Add**

Click **OK**

Or, click **New Contact** and enter the required information to add someone to the group and to your Address Book. Click **Add** and **OK** when you are done.

To Send a Message to a Group with the Address Book

The long way...

Open a new message.

Click on the Address Book icon next to the **To** or **Cc** field.

Click on the group on the left side of the **Select Recipients** box. (I clicked on "My Gang" here):

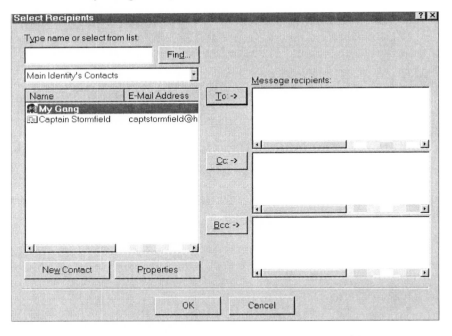

Click *My Gang*, and then click *To* to address a message to this group.

Click the **To, Cc,** or **Bcc** field button. Your selected group will move into the Message Recipients field.

Click **OK** to address the message.

The easy way...

Just type the name of the group into the New Message address field!

In summary, Outlook Express has many attractive features. It is a powerful program, and will take more time to become accustomed to, in its intricacies, than most Web-based mail systems. It is, however, well worth considering as the system of choice for those who anticipate doing extensive emailing. If you make Outlook Express your choice, do be sure to consult the Microsoft sites noted above to stay abreast of discovered security glitches and fixes.

Index

193